Programming in C

Suresh L, Chandrakant Naikodi & Badrinath G Srinivas

Programming in C

Published by White Falcon Publishing
No. 335, Sector - 48 A
Chandigarh - 160047

ISBN - 978-1-943851-68-3

ABOUT AUTHOR

- Dr. Suresh L

  Dr. Suresh L, Principal of CiTech, is ambitious and has been an eminent achiever throughout his service. He has over 24 years of teaching and administration experience. He is a source of inspiration for all the Cambrians, both faculties and students. He is a path setter for the development of both students and faculties. He is instrumental in conducting all college activities successfully. Apart from being a able leader, he is recognized as an eminent teacher. He is a member of Board of Studies / Examiners for various universities and autonomous Institutions. He has visited many countries like Singapore, Malaysia, Poland, Australia, UAE and Greece for academic pursuits. He gave Key Note address in the IEEE conference at Singapore. He is a Life member of ISTE and CSI and member of IEEE. He has published over 50 papers in National and International conferences and Journals. His current areas of interest include Data mining, Database Management Systems, Cloud Computing and Big Data. He had been a member of recruitment committees and resource person for many corporate companies.

- Dr. Chandrakant Naikodi

  Dr. Chandrakant Naikodi is presently working as a Project Leader in MNC., Bangalore, India. He has received B.E. degree from the Visvesvaraya Technological University, Karnataka, India in 2004, and M.E. and Ph.D(CSE) degrees from Bangalore University, India in 2006 and 2014 respectively. His research interests include Computer Networks, MANETs, WSN, Programming Languages, Big Data and Databases. He has published many research papers in referred International Journals and Conferences. Also, he is the author of five technical books titled "C:Test Your Aptitude" and "1000 Questions and Answers in C++" published by Tata Mc-Graw Hill and other technical books titled "Programming in C and Data Structure", "Managing Big Data" and "Introduction to Computing and Problem Solving" by Vikas Publication which are widely used in both industry and academia. He has published over 50 papers in International Conferences and Journals.

- Dr. Badrinath G. Srinivas

  Dr Badrinath G. Srinivas is presently working as a Development Manager in Samsung India Electronics Pvt Ltd, India. He has received B.E. degree from the Visvesvaraya Technological University, Karnataka, India in 2003. He has received M.E. and Ph.D. degrees from Bangalore University, India in 2005 and Indian Institute of Technology Kanpur, India in 2012 respectively. His research interests include Biometrics, Pattern recognition, Computer Vision, Large Data Classification and Indexing for efficient searching, Human Computer Interface, Graphical and Gesture based authentication techniques robust to shoulder surfing and Wireless Networks. He has published many conference and journal articles in premium forums. He has also published four patents on authentication techniques robust shoulder security and human interface for audio files.

PREFACE

- These days IT communities of Computer Science are encouraged to dive into different languages and C language stands first among them. The C language is one of the popular Computer Language, it has its own standard specifications. This book concentrates on C introduction, syntaxes, examples,etc.

Dedicating to users of this book....

Contents

Chapter 1

INTRODUCTION to C LANGUAGE

What is a computer?

A computer is an electronic device capable of performing computations and making logical decisions at extremely speed which is multiple times quicker than human beings. Using computer programs, computers process data under the control of instructions sets. There are set of a variety of devices such as keyboard, screen, disks, memory and processing units that consist of a computer systems are referred to as hardware. The computer program that runs on a computer is called as software.

In 1945, Von Neumann(Newman) architecture/model illustrates a design architecture for an electronic digital computer with parts having of a Central Processing Unit(CPU) which includes processor registers and an arithmetic logic unit, a control unit holding an instruction register and program counter, external mass storage, a memory need to store both data and instructions, and input and output devices. Von Neumann(Newman) architecture/model is shown in Figure 15.1. Any stored-program computer in which an instruction fetch and a data operation cannot occur together because they share a common bus. This is called to as the Von Neumann bottleneck and usually restricts the performance of the system.

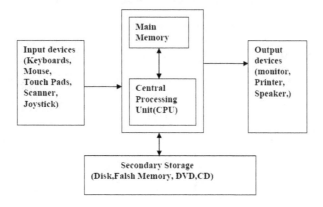

Figure 1.1 Von Neumann(Newman)'s Computer Architecture/Model

Von Neumann model design is simpler than the more modern Harvard architecture which is also a stored-program system but has one dedicated address set and data buses for reading data from and writing data to memory and another address set and data buses for fetching instructions.

1

1.1 ELECTRONIC COMPUTERS THEN AND NOW

The first computer was built in the late 1930s by Dr.John Atanasoff and Clifford Berry at USA's Iowa State University. They premeditated their computer to assist graduate students in nuclear physics with their mathematical calculations.

ENIAC(Electronic Numerical Integrator And Computer) is a first large-scale, general purpose electronic digital computer completed in 1946 at the University of Pennsylvania with funding from the US army.

In the beginning, computers were used vacuum tubes as their basic electronic components. Nowadays new generations of computers were significantly faster, smaller and less costly than earlier ones. By means of today's technology, the entire circuitry of a computer processor can be grouped in a single electronic component called a computer/microprocessor chip. These chips are installed in PDS's (Personal Digital Assistance), GPS systems, cameras, watches, home appliances, automobiles, and certainly computers.

Nowadays computers are categorized according to their size and performance. Personal computers are meant for a single person and Mainframes are large , very powerful used for real-time transaction processing systems, banking networks, motels, ATMs reservations systems for airline, etc.. Supercomputers are having largest capacity and fastest computers which is used by research laboratories and computationally number crunching application such as weather forecasting. Computer system elements fall into two major categories: Hardware and Software. Hardware is the equipment used to perform the mandatory computations and includes the Central Processing Unit(CPU), monitor, keyboard, printer, memories, mouse, and speaker. Software consist of the programs that permit us to solve problems with computer by providing it with lists of instruction to carry out.

1.2 COMPUTER HARDWARE

Von Neumann computer systems has three important building blocks: CPU, Memory and Input/Output devices (I/O). All these components are connected through system bus, the most prominent items within the CPU are the registers which can be manipulated directly by a computer program.

Components of the Von Neumann Model includes below parts,

1. Memory: It stores the information (data/program)

2. Processing Unit: CPU used for Computation/Processing of Information

3. Input: Getting data into the computer. e.g. keyboard, mouse

4. Output: Getting data out of the computer. e.g. printer, monitor

5. Control Unit: Makes sure that all the other parts perform their tasks accurately and at the correct time

The CPU contains three main components, they are, one or more Arithmetic Logic Units, (ALUs)Control Unit (CU) and different registers. The CU follows the order in which instructions should be executed and controls the retrieval of the suitable operands and it interprets the system. CU produces sequence of control signals for each instruction execution. Basically; the CU presides over the flow of data through the machine by passing control signals to different components. A micro-operation (MO) is a operation produced by a control signal. The basic operations of ALUs is to carry out all mathematical and Boolean operations.

Registers are often resides on the same chip and directly connected to the CU which comprise faster access time than memory. Hence registers are used to speedily store and transfer the data and instructions being used. So, registers are used as as the source of operands and as the destination of results will get better the performance. A CPU specifically implemented on a single chip is called a microprocessor.

Computer memory is used to store instructions and data of program. We can classify memory into two types; they are RAM (random-access memory) and ROM (read-only memory). RAM stores the data and general-purpose programs that the machine executes. RAM is momentary; that is, its contents can be changed at any time and it is erasing when power to the computer is turned off. ROM is permanent and is used to store the initial boot up instructions of the machine.

The I/O interfaces perform operations to get data and send data to output devices. In addition, they permit the computer to communicate to the user and to secondary storage devices like tape and disk drives. All these devices are connected to each other through a signal lines collection known as a bus. Main buses carrying data are the control bus, data bus and address bus. Every bus has numerous wires that permit for the parallel transmission of data between varieties of hardware components. Address bus recognizes either a memory location or an I/O device. The data bus, which is bidirectional, sends data to/from a component. The control bus has signals that allow the CPU to communicate with the memory and I/O devices.

Von Neumann machine needs the use of the three main components just described above. Typically, a software package, called an Operating System (OS), controls how these three components work together. At first, a program has to be loaded into the memory, prior being loaded; the program is typically stored on a secondary storage device (e.g., disk). The OS uses the I/O interfaces to retrieve the program from secondary storage and load it into the memory. Once the program is in memory, the OS then schedules the CPU to start executing the program instructions. Each instruction to be executed should first be retrieved from memory. This retrieval is referred to as an instruction fetch. Following an instruction is fetched; it is put into a special register in the CPU, called the instruction register (IR). As in the IR, the instruction is decoded to determine what type of operation should be carrying out. If the instruction needs operands, these are fetched from memory or possibly from other registers and placed into the correct location. The instruction is then carried out and the results are stored back into memory and/or registers. This process is repetitive for each instruction of the program until the end of program is reached.

1.2.1 Memory

System memory stores data, instructions needed while processing data and output results. Storage may be required for short time and long time. Memory is classified based on its purpose and features. The cache memory, RAM and registers are fast memories used to store the data and instructions temporarily while processing. Secondary memory includes magnetic tape/disks, optical disks which has large storage to store data and instructions permanently. But these memories have slow performance compare to primary memory.

Memory Representation:

Unit	Size
1 bit	0/1 bit
1 byte	8 bits
1KB(Kilobyte)	1024bytes
1MB(Megabyte)	1024KB
1GB(Gigabyte)	1024MB
1TB(Terbyte)	1024GB

Table 1.1 Memory Measurement Units

Memory should support to store input data, output data, intermediate results, processing data, instructions etc. The basic unit of memory is *binary digit/bit* which is a single binary value 0 or 1. A bit is the smallest unit to represent computer data. Computer forms bits group with 8 bits called a *byte*. One byte can store 256 bits of different combinations starts from 00000000 to 11111111. Again group of bytes called as *word* which is a 2/4/8 bytes size. Table 11.1 shows list of all memory measurements.

Computer memory is logically organized as a linear array of locations. The range of the memory addresses is O to maximum size of memory for a processor. Memory is characterized on basis of capacity and access time. Where capacity is the amount of information/data that a memory can store. Access time is the time interval between read/write request and the availability of data. Lesser the access time, the faster is the speed of memory. The cost of the memory is high if speed and largest capacity required. The hierarchy of the different memory types is shown in Figure 1.2.

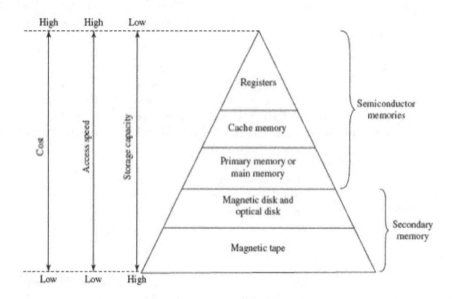

Figure 1.2 Computer Memory Hierarchy

Two broad categories of memory are internal and external memories. The internal memory consists of the CPU registers, cache memory and primary memory. External memory or secondary memory is used to store large amount of data/information.

Key features of Internal Memory:
a. Limited storage capacity
b. Temporary storage
c. Fast access
d. High cost
e. Example:Register, Cache, primary memory(RAM/ROM)

Key features of secondary memory:
a. Very hight storage capacity
b. Permanent storage(non-volatile) unless erased by user
c. Relatively slower access
d. Stores data/instructions used by CPU
e. Cheapest among all memory

CPU Registers:
Registers are very high speed storage areas located inside the CPU. The data and instructions are moved to the registers for processing after CPU gets the data and instructions from the cache/RAM. Hence it is called as *working memory*. The more number of registers and bigger the size of each register, the better it is.
Cache Memory:

Cache memory is a fast memory placed in between the CPU and the RAM. It is a faster than RAM. When the CPU requires an instruction/data during processing, it first finds at cache. If it is present in the cache then it takes called as cache hit else called as cache miss then taken it from RAM.

Primary Memory:

It is a main memory of system, it can be classified into two types- RAM(Random Access Memory) and ROM(Read Only Memory). It is a computer storage location that permits data to be stored and accessed fast from random locations within DRAM(Dynamic Random Access Memory is one of the most commonly found RAM modules in PC compatible personal computers.) on a memory portion. Since data is accessed randomly instead of sequentially like it is on a CD/hard drive, the computer can access the data much faster. However, unlike ROM and the hard drive RAM is a volatile memory and needs power in order to keep the data accessible, if power is lost all data contained in memory lost.

When the computer boots up, parts of the OS and drivers are loaded into memory, which permits the CPU to process the instructions much faster, so taking less time before our system is operational. After the OS has loaded, each program you open such as the browser you are using to view this page is loaded into memory while it is running.

ROM is a computer memory on which data has been pre-recorded. Once data has been written onto a ROM chip, it cannot be deleted and can only be read. Unlike main memory (RAM), ROM retains its contents even when the computer is turned off. ROM is referred to as being non-volatile memory, whereas RAM is volatile. Many personal computers have a small size of ROM that stores important programs such as the program that boots the computer. ROMs are used extensively in calculators and peripheral devices such as laser printers.

Secondary Memory:

Data in primary memory must be saved to secondary memory(disks and tape), storage needed to keep data into memory. Two types of secondary memory - sequential and direct access. Sequential access like audio tapes used to access sequentially, say listen to track 5, we have to pass tracks 1,2,3,4.

Direct access like hard disk/flash drive, file allocation table permits us to seek to an exact file without having to pass over any previous ones. Magnetic tape is a medium for magnetic recording, made of a thin magnetizable coating on a long, narrow strip of plastic film. It is based on magnetic wire recording. Devices that record and play back audio and video using magnetic tape are tape recorders and video tape recorders. Magnetic disk is a primary computer storage device. Like tape, it is magnetically recorded and can be re-recorded over and over. Disks are rotating platters with a mechanical arm that moves a read/write head between the outer and inner edges of the surface of platter. It can take as long as one second to find a location on a floppy disk to as little as a couple of milliseconds on a fast hard disk. The disk surface is divided into concentric tracks. The thinner the tracks, the more storage. The data bits are recorded as tiny magnetic spots on the tracks. The smaller the spot, the more bits per inch and the greater the storage.

A floppy disk is magnetic storage medium for computer systems. The floppy disk is composed of a thin and flexible magnetic disk sealed in a square plastic carrier. To read and write data from a floppy disk, a computer system must have a floppy disk drive (FDD). Early days of personal computing, floppy disks were widely used to distribute software, transfer files and create back-up copies of data. When hard drives were still very expensive, floppy disks were also used to store the OS of a computer. Hard disks can store more data and are faster than floppy disks. A hard disk, for example, can store anywhere from 10 to more than 1000 gigabytes, whereas most floppies have a maximum storage capacity of 1.4 megabytes.

A single hard disk generally consists of many platters. Each platter requires two read/write heads, one for each side. All the read/write heads are attached to a single access arm so that they cannot move independently. Each platter has the same number of tracks, and a track location that cuts across all platters is called a cylinder, HDD is shown in Figure 1.3.

Compared the hard disk with floppy disk:

1. Hard disks store much more data per square inch of recording surface.

2. The hard disks to have more tracks per radial inch and to write more bits per inch along each track.

3. Hard disks can transfer data faster than floppy disks.

4. Access times are also faster for hard disks than floppy disks.

5. Floppy disks are transportable while the hard disk is not transportable.

6. HDD tend to be noisier than floppy disk drives.

7. HDD is more sensitivity than floppy disks.

8. The hard disk drives cost much higher than floppy disk drives.

Zip disks are slightly bigger than conventional floppy disks and about twice as thick. They can hold 100 or 250 MB of data. Because they're relatively inexpensive and durable, they have become a popular media for backing up hard disks and for transporting large files.

An optical disc is an electronic data storage medium that can be written to and read using a low-powered laser beam. Stored data as micron-wide dots of light and dark. A laser read the dots, and the data was converted to an electrical signal, and finally to audio or visual output. However, the technology didn't appear in the marketplace until Philips and Sony came out with the compact disc (CD) in 1982. Since then, there has been a constant succession of optical disc formats, first in CD formats, followed by a number of DVD formats.

A CD-ROM is a pre-pressed optical compact disc which contains information. The name is an acronym which stands for "Compact Disc Read-Only Memory". Computers can read CD-ROMs(compact disk-read only memory), but cannot write to CD-ROMs which are not writable or erasable. Nowadays we can do read/write on these discs.

Digital versatile disc-read only memory (DVD-ROM) is a read-only digital versatile disc (DVD) commonly used for storing large software applications. It is similar to a compact disk-read only memory (CD-ROM) but has a bigger capacity. A DVD-ROM stores upto 4.7 GB of data. A CD-ROM usually stores 650 MB of data. A DVD-ROM permanently stores data files which cannot be changed, written over or erased. A personal

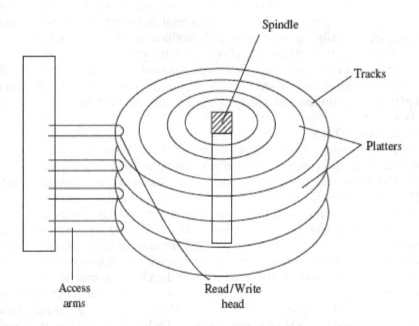

Figure 1.3 Parts of Hard Disk

computer (PC) with a DVD-ROM or a DVD-RAM drive is designed to read a DVD-ROM disc. Generally a DVD-ROM disc is not equipped to be used with a DVD drive connected to a home theater system or television. But many DVD-ROM drives can typically read a DVD movie disc. Compared to a CD-ROM, a DVD-ROM has the same 5 inch diameter and 1.2 millimeter (mm) thickness. But because a DVD-ROM uses a shorter wavelength laser with tighter compacted pits, the disc capacity is increased. In fact, the smallest DVD-ROM can store around 7 times more data than a CD-ROM.

I/O is one of the component of system which has input unit and output unit. Input unit does feeding data into system and output does accepting data from system.

1.2.2 Input

Listed few of the important input devices: Keyboard, Mouse, Joy Stick, Light pen, Track Ball, Scanner, Graphic Tablet, Microphone, Magnetic Ink Card Reader (MICR), Optical Character Reader (OCR), Bar Code Reader, Optical Mark Reader(OMR), Keyboard.

1. Keyboard : Keyboard is the most general and very popular input device which facilitates in inputting data to the system. A keyboard looks like a typewriter, although there are some additional keys provided for performing additional functions. Keyboards are of two sizes 84 keys or 101/102 keys, but now keyboards with 104 keys or 108 keys are also existing for Windows and Internet.

2. Mouse: Mouse is most well-liked pointing device. It is very well-known cursor-control devices have a small palm size box with a round ball at its base which senses the mouse movement and passes equivalent signals to CPU when the buttons of mouse pushed. Usually it has two buttons called right and left button and a wheel is placed between the buttons. Mouse can be used to control the cursor location on screen, but it cannot be used to enter text into the computer, however you can use for copy and paste operation. Its advantages includes, not very expensive, easy to use and moves the cursor faster than the keyboard's arrow keys.

3. Joystick: Joystick is also a pointing device like mouse which is used to move cursor position on a screen of monitor. Joystick is basically a stick having a spherical ball at its both upper and lower ends. The lower spherical ball moves in a socket. The joystick can be moved in all 4 directions. The joystick function is alike to that of a mouse. It is largely used in CAD(Computer Aided Designing) and playing games in computer.

4. Light Pen: It is a pointing device which is alike to a pen. Light pen is used to select a displayed menu item/draw images on the screen of monitor. It contains a photocell and an optical system placed in a small tube. When the light pen's tip is moved over the monitor screen and pen button is pushed, its photocell sensing element detects the screen location and passes the equivalent signal to the CPU.

5. Track Ball: This is also an input device that is mainly used in laptop or notebook/computer, in its place of a mouse. This ball is half inserted and by moving fingers on ball, pointer on screen can be moved. As the entire device is not moved, a track ball needs less space compare to a mouse. Track ball comes in a variety of shapes like a ball a square and a button.

6. Scanner: It is an input device which works more similar to a photocopy machine. Scanner is used when some data is available on a paper and used to be transferred to the computer's hard disc for additional manipulation. The scanner captures pictures from the source which are then converted into the digital form that can be stored on the disc. Such pictures can be altered prior they are printed.

7. Digitizer: This device converts analog data into digital form. It can convert a signal from the camera/TV into a series of numbers that could be stored in a system. It can be consumed by the system to create a image of whatever the camera had been pointed at. Digitizer is also recognized as Graphics Tablet or just Tablet since it transforms graphics and graphic data into binary inputs. Graphic tablet as digitizer is used for doing fine works of drawing and image alteration applications.

8. Microphone: It is used to get the input sound that is then converted into a digital form. Microphone is used for a variety of applications like adding sound to a multimedia presentation or for mixing music.

9. Magnetic Ink Card Reader(MICR): MICR is a input device which is usually used in banks because of a large number of cheques to be processed in day by day activities. The code number of bank and cheque number are printed on the cheques with a particular type of ink that has particles of magnetic material that are machine readable. The process of reading is called Magnetic Ink Character Recognition (MICR). The main advantages of MICR is that it is less error prone and it is fast.

10. Optical Character Reader(OCR): The OCR is an input device used to read a printed text. It scans text optically character by character, transforms them into a machine readable code and stores the text on the system memory.

11. Bar Code Readers: It is a device used for reading bar coded data. Bar coded data is usually used in labelling goods, numbering the books, toys, etc. It may be embedded in a stationary scanner or may be a hand held scanner. Bar Code Reader scans a bar code picture/image, transforms it into an alphanumeric value which is then fed to the system to which bar code reader is connected.

12. Optical Mark Reader(OMR): The OMR is a unique type of optical scanner used to recognize the type of mark made by pencil or pen. It is used where one out of a few substitutes is to be chosen and marked. It is specially used for checking the answer sheets of examinations having multiple choice questions(MCQ).

1.2.3   Output

Monitors, Graphic Plotter and Printer are few among of the important output devices which are used in a system.

1. Monitors: Monitors usually called as Visual Display Unit (VDU), is a main output device of a computer. It structures images from tiny dots, called pixels; the sharpness of the image depends upon the number of pixels. There are two kinds of presentation screen used for monitors, Cathode-Ray Tube (CRT) and Flat- Panel Display.
Cathode-Ray Tube (CRT) Monitor:
The CRT display is made up of pixels which is a small picture element. The smaller the pixels, the better the image precision/resolution. It obtains more than one illuminated pixel to form whole character, such as the letter a' in the word help. A preset number of characters can be displayed on a screen at once. The screen can be split into a series of character boxes - fixed location on the screen where a standard character can be placed. Nowadays most screens are proficient of displaying 80 characters of data horizontally and 25 lines vertically. There are some disadvantages of CRT, they are, CRT consumes more energy and it is large in size.
Flat-Panel Display Monitor:
The flat-panel display refers to a class of video devices that have solid volume, less weight and less power necessity in comparison to the CRT. We can hang up them on walls or wear them on your wrists. Current uses of flat-panel displays include calculators, monitors, laptop, graphics display, computer and video games. The flat-panel display is classified into two categories: first is, Emissive Displays - this transforms electrical energy into light. Examples are LED(Light-Emitting Diodes) and plasma panel. Second is, Non-Emissive Displays it uses optical effects to transform light/sunlight from some other source into graphics patterns. Example is LCD(Liquid-Crystal Device).

2. Printers: Printer is an output device, which is used to print the data on paper. There are two types of printers: Impact Printers and Non-Impact Printers.
Impact Printers:
The impact printers print the characters by striking them on the ribbon which is then pressed on the paper. Features of Impact Printers are: very noisy, very little consumable costs, helpful for bulk printing due to low cost and there is physical contact with the paper to produce an image.

These printers are of two types: Character printers and Line printers.

Character Printers:

Character printers are the printers which print one character at a time. These are further divided into two types: Dot Matrix Printer (DMP) and Daisy Wheel. The Dot Matrix Printer printers are popular because of their ease of printing and economical price. Each character printed is in form of pattern of dots and head consists of a Matrix of Pins of size (5*7, 7*9, 9*7 or 9*9) which comes out to form a character that is why it is called Dot Matrix Printer. Advantages of DMP are, reasonably priced, extensively used and Other language characters can be printed. Disadvantages include Poor Quality and Slow Speed. In Daisy Wheel, head is lying on a wheel and pins corresponding to characters are like petals of Daisy (flower name) that is why it is called Daisy Wheel Printer. These printers are typically used for word-processing in offices which want a few letters to be sent here and there with very nice quality. Advantages include, better quality, more reliable than DMP and fonts of character can be easily changed. Disadvantages include, noisy, slower than DMP and more costly than DMP.

Line Printers:

These printers print one line at a time. Line printers classified into two types, Drum Printer and Chain Printer.

Drum Printer is like a drum in shape so it is called drum printer. The surface of drum is partitioned into number of tracks. Total tracks are equal to the paper size i.e. for a paper width of 132 characters, drum will have 132 tracks. A character set is imprinted on track. The different character sets accessible in the market are 48, 64 and 96 characters set. One rotation of drum prints one line. Drum printers are express in speed and can print 300 to 2000 lines per minute. Advantages of Drum Printer include very high speed and disadvantages include characters fonts cannot be changed, very expensive.

In Chain Printer, character sets are used which is a standard character set may have 48/64/96 characters. Disadvantages include, it is noisy. Advantages include character fonts can easily be changed and different languages can be used with the same printer.

Non-impact Printers:

Printing the characters without using ribbon is called Non-impact printers. These printers print a whole page in single attempt hence they are also known as Page Printers. Non-impact printers are classified into two types, Laser Printers and Inkjet Printers.

Characteristics of Non-impact Printers, they are not noisy, quicker than impact printers, high quality, support many fonts and different character size.

Laser Printers:

These are non-impact page printers. Laser Printers use laser lights to make the dots required to form the characters to be printed on a page. Advantages include, gives good graphics quality, very high quality output, very high speed and support many fonts and different character size. Disadvantages include, costly and cannot be used to generate multiple copies of a document in a sole printing.

Inkjet Printers:

Inkjet printers are non-impact character printers based on a moderately recent technology. Inkjet print characters by spraying small ink drops onto paper. They create high quality output with presentable features. They make less noise since no hammering is done and these have many styles of printing modes available. Colour printing is also achievable. Some models of Inkjet printers can generate multiple copies of printing also. Advantages of Inkjet include more reliable and high quality printing. Disadvantages include, costly as cost per page is high and slow as matched up to laser printer.

1.3 COMPUTER SOFTWARE

Software can be classified in two ways in a computer. These are Operating system(OS) and Application software. First is, Operating System which is a collection of computer programs that control interaction of user and computer. Second is, application programs which are developed to assist a computer user in accomplishing specific task. For example , a word-processing application MS Word etc.

Computer software is made of one or more computer programs written in one of computer language type. Sometimes it means one specific program, or it can mean all the software on a system, including the applications and OS. Applications are programs that do a specific business, such as a game or a word processor, ATM transaction etc.

Computer software includes computer programs, libraries and their related documentation. Software is also sometimes called as application software . At the lowest level, executable code consists of machine language instructions precise to an individual processor usually a CPU. A machine language has groups of binary values signifying processor instructions that change the state of the computer from its preceding state.

Software written in a machine language is known as "machine code". However, nowadays, software is usually written in high-level programming languages that are easier and more efficient for humans to use (closer to natural language) than machine language. High-level languages are translated, using compilation or interpretation or a combination of the two, into machine language. Software may also be written in a low-level assembly language, fundamentally, a vaguely mnemonic representation of a machine language using a natural language alphabet. Assembly language is translated into machine code using an assembler.

1.3.1 Operating System(OS)

An operating system (OS) is software that manages computer hardware and software resources and offers common services for computer programs. The layers and views of a computer system is shown in Figure 1.4. The operating system is an fundamental component of the system software in a computer system. Application programs typically need an OS to function.

Time-sharing OS schedule tasks for efficient use of the system and may also contain accounting software for cost allocation of processor time, printing, mass storage and other resources.

For hardware functions such as input and output and memory allocation, the OS acts as an mediator between programs and the computer hardware, although the application code is typically executed directly by the hardware and frequently makes system calls to an OS function or be interrupted by it. The OSs are found on many devices that contain a computer from cellular phones and video game consoles to web servers and supercomputers.

Examples of well-known modern OSs include Microsoft Windows, Android, BlackBerry 10, BSD, Chrome OS, iOS, Linux, OS X, QNX, Windows Phone, and z/OS.

Objectives of operating systems:

A program that controls the execution of application programs. An interface between applications and hardware. The following are the objectives of operating system,

Convenience: Makes the computer more expedient to use

Efficiency: Permits computer system resources to be used in an efficient way

Ability to evolve: Allow effective development, testing, and introduction of new system functions without intrusive with service

Basically OS is a program that mediates between application programs and the hardware, a set of procedures that enable a group of people to use a computer system. A program that controls the execution of application programs and it acts as an interface between applications and hardware.

1.4 ALGORITHM

Algorithm are the set of well defined instruction in sequence to solve a program. An algorithm should always have a clear end point.

Certain qualities of a good algorithm are listed below,

a). Inputs and outputs must be defined precisely.

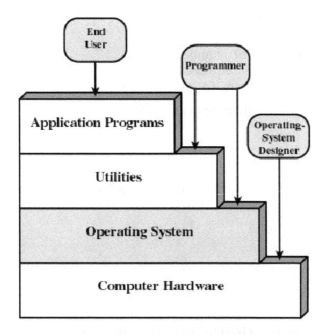

Figure 1.4 Computer System's Layers

b). Each steps in algorithm must be clear and unambiguous.

c). Algorithm should be most effective among many different ways to solve a problem.

d). An algorithm must not have computer code. Instead, the algorithm should be written in such a way that, it can be used in similar programming languages.

Examples: Write an algorithm to add two numbers entered by user.

Step 1: Start

Step 2: Declare variables num1, num2 and sum.

Step 3: Read values num1 and num2.

Step 4: Add num1 and num2 and assign the result to sum. sum←num1+num2

Step 5: Display sum

Step 6: Stop

Writing comfortable high-level statements of a C program or algorithm intended for human reading rather than machine reading. Pseudocode is used as a problem-solving tool which acts as intermediate step(s) between English and C program. This is most acceptable procedure because it helps programmers to translate English to C.

How to solve a problem? First requirement is to list a set of steps (algorithm) which describe the operations necessary to obtain the solution.

When you get a problem, try to solve below questions,

(a) Carefully read the problem and understand what exactly expected to do?

(b) What outputs/answers to be printed?

(c) What are the steps to translate a problem from English to C?

(d) If a problem is too big, then check weather it is possible to break into pieces?

Lets take a program: Display numbers from 4 to 9 and square it after each number.

Pseudocode example of this program,

```
Step 1: Start from number 4
Step 2: Calculate the square of number
Step 3: Display number and its square
Step 4: Do this step for all remain numbers
```

Above code can generate output for a given input as follows.

```
Input :4  5  6  7  8  9
Output:16  25  36  49  64  81
```

Another example, read N number and print 2 power of N. The Pseudocode would be,

```
Step 1: Read N.
Step 2: Initialize power to 1.
Step 3: Repeat N times:
Step 4: Double power.
Step 5: End repeat
Step 6: Write power.
Step 7: Stop.
```

One way to categorize algorithms is by implementation, they are

(i) Recursion or iteration: A recursive algorithm invokes itself repetitively until a definite condition matches, which is a method general to functional programming. Iterative algorithms use recurring constructs like loops and sometimes supplementary data structures like stacks to solve the particular problems. Some problems are as usual suited for one implementation or the other. For example, a tower of Hanoi is well understood using recursive implementation. Every recursive version has an equivalent iterative version, and vice versa.

(ii) Logical: An algorithm may be viewed as controlled logical presumption. This notion may be expressed as: Algorithm = logic + control. The logic component states the axioms that may be used in the computation and the control component determines the way in which deduction is applied to the axioms. This is the base for the logic programming paradigm. In pure logic programming languages the control component is fixed and algorithms are specified by supplying only the logic component. The insist of this approach is the stylish semantics: a change in the axioms has a precise change in the algorithm.

(iii) Serial, parallel or distributed: Algorithms are normally discussed with the assumption that computers execute one instruction of an algorithm at a time called serial computers. An algorithm designed for such an situation is called a serial algorithm, as opposed to parallel algorithms or distributed algorithms. Parallel algorithms take advantage of computer architectures where many processors can work on a problem simultaneously, whereas distributed algorithms use multiple machines connected with a network. Distributed or parallel algorithms divide the problem into more symmetrical or asymmetrical sub-problems and get together the results back together. The resource utilization in such algorithms is not only processor cycles on each processor but also the communication overhead between the processors. A few sorting algorithms can be parallelized efficiently, but their communication overhead is costly. Iterative algorithms are usually parallelizable. A few problems have no parallel algorithms and are called intrinsically serial problems.

(iv) Deterministic or non-deterministic: Deterministic algorithms determine the problem with precise decision at every step of the algorithm whereas non-deterministic algorithms solve problems through guessing although normal guesses are made more precise through the use of heuristics.

(v) Exact or approximate: While many algorithms reach a precise solution, rough calculation algorithms seek an approximation that is close to the true solution. Estimate may use either a deterministic or a random strategy. Such algorithms have practical value for many hard problems.

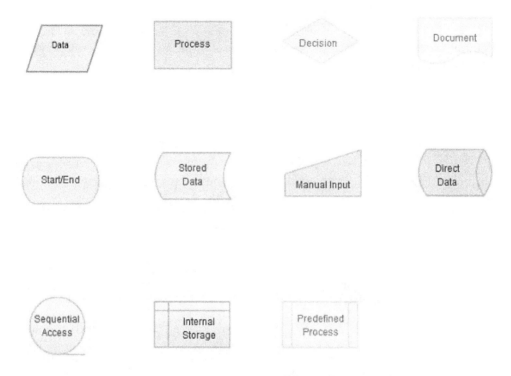

Figure 1.5 Flowchart Symbols

1.5 FLOWCHARTS

Flowchart is a diagram of the sequence of movements or actions of people or things involved in a complex system or activity. It is a graphical representation of a computer program in relation to its sequence of functions. A flowchart is a visual depiction, which shows you a sequence of operations that are to be performed in order to get the solution to a problem. While flowcharts may be applied to computer solutions, they are an excellent tool when it comes to business, education and even something as innumerable as a formula or a how-to guide. Not really understanding flowchart symbols is surely something that could leave you in a quandary, particularly if you are not too aware of the relevance of flowcharting symbols. Figure 14.10 shows standard symbols along with a visual representation:

(i) Data object - Often called as the I/O Shape that shows the Inputs to and Outputs from a process.

(ii) Rectangle - Rectangle is used to represent an event which is controlled within the process. Normally this will be a step or action which is taken.

(iii) Diamond It is used to symbolize a decision point in the process. Usually, the statement in the symbol will require a yes' or no' response and branch to different parts of the flowchart accordingly.

(iv) Document - The Document object is a rectangle with a wave-like base. This shape is used to characterize a Document or Report in a process flow.

(v) Rounded box This is used to symbolize an event which happens involuntarily. Such an event will trigger a subsequent action, for example 'receive telephone call, or describe a new state of affairs.

(vi) Stored data - This is a common data storage object used in the process flow as opposed to data which could be also stored on a magnetic tape, hard drive, memory card, of any other storage device.

(vii) Manual input - This object is characterized by rectangle with the top sloping up from left to right. Manual Input object signifies an action where the user is prompted for information that should be manually input into a system.

(viii) Direct data Direct data object in a process flow stands for information stored which can be accessed directly. This object represents a hard drive of computer.

(ix) Circle It is used to represent a point at which the flowchart connects with another process. The name or reference for the other process should show within the symbol.

(x) Internal storage This is an object which is usually found in programming flowcharts to demonstrate the information stored in memory, as opposed to on a file.

(xi) Predefined process This permits you to write one subroutine and call it as often as you like from anywhere in the code.

While learning a variety of symbols that are associated with flowcharts are rather important, you require to also remember that there are certain guidelines in flowcharting that deserves some respect as well. The following are some guiding principles in flowcharting:

(i) Proper Form is Essential: While drawing a proper flowchart, all necessary needs should be listed out in logical order.

(ii) Clarity is Paramount: The flowchart should be plain, neat and easy to follow. There should not be any room for doubt in understanding the flowchart.

(iii) Stick to the Right Direction: The general direction of the flow of a procedure or system is from left to right or top to bottom.

(iv) Standard for Flow Lines: If possible just one flow line should come out from a process symbol. While only one flow line should enter a decision symbol, around three flow lines (depending on the answer) should leave the decision symbol. In addition, only one flow line is making use of together with a terminal symbol.

(v) Be brief, not bountiful: Write within standard symbols in a few words.

(vi) Logic precedes everything: If you are dealing with a complex flowchart then use connector symbols to reduce the number of flow lines. Ditch the intersection of flow lines to make certain effectiveness and healthier communication. It is imperative that your flowchart has a logical start and finish.

1.6   SOFTWARE DEVELOPMENT METHOD

A software development method in software engineering is a part of software development work into distinct phases/stages consist of activities with the intent of better planning and management. It is often considered a subset of the systems development life cycle. The methodology may have the pre-definition of specific deliverables and artifacts that are created and completed by a project team to develop/maintain an application.

General methodologies include waterfall, iterative, prototyping and incremental development, spiral development, rapid application development, extreme programming and many other types of agile methodology. In some cases, we consider a life-cycle "model" a more usual term for a category of methodologies and a software development "process" a more specific term to refer to a specific process chosen by a specific organization. For example, there are many specific software development processes that fit the spiral life-cycle model.

1.7   APPLYING THE SOFTWARE DEVELOPMENT METHOD

Since many years a range of frameworks have advanced over the years, each has its own recognized weaknesses and strengths. One software development methodology framework is not essentially appropriate for use by all projects. Each one of the available methodology frameworks are greatest suited to explicit kinds of projects, based on a variety of technical, project, organizational and team deliberations.

Software development organizations implement process methodologies to easiness the development process. Occasionally, contractors may need methodologies employed, an example is the U.S. defense industry, which needs a rating based on process models to get contracts. The global standard for describing the method of selecting, implementing and monitoring the life cycle for software is ISO/IEC 12207.

A decades-long objective has been to find repeatable, expected processes that improve productivity and quality. A variety of try to systematize or formalize the seemingly disorderly task of designing software. Others apply project management techniques to design software. Without effective project management, software projects can simply be delivered late or over financial plan. With large numbers of software projects not meeting their expectations in terms of functionality, cost, or delivery schedule, it is effective project management that becomes visible to be lacking.

Organizations may create a Software Engineering Process Group (SEPG), which is the crucial point for process improvement. Composed of line practitioners who have diverse skills, the group is at the centre of the collaborative effort of everyone in the organization who is occupied with software engineering process improvement.

A particular development team can also agree to programming environment details, such as which integrated development environment is used, and one or more dominant programming paradigms, programming style rules, or selection of specific software libraries or software frameworks. These details are usually not dictated by the selection of model or common methodology.

1.8   PSEUDOCODE SOLUTION TO PROBLEM

Pseudocode is a notation resembling a simplified programming language which is used in program design. Pseudocode can be used as a problem-solving tool for any kind of algorithms, basically Pseudocode acts as intermediate step(s) between C program and English. This is most acceptable procedure because it helps programmers to translate English to C.

How to solve a problem? First necessity is to list a set of steps (algorithm) which explains the operations needed to have the solution.

When you get a problem, try to solve below questions,

(a) Carefully read the problem and understand what exactly expected to do?

(b) What outputs/answers to be printed?

(c) What are the steps to translate a problem from English to C?

(d) If a problem is too big, then check weather it is possible to break into pieces?

Lets take a program: Display numbers from 4 to 9 and square it after each number.
Pseudocode example of this program,

```
Step  1:  Start  from  number  4
Step  2:  Calculate  the  square  of  number
Step  3:  Display  number  and  its  square
Step  4:  Do  this  step  for  all  remain  numbers
```

Above code can generate output for a given input as follows.

```
Input :4   5   6   7   8   9
Output:16  25  36  49  64  81
```

Another example, read N number and print 2 power of N. The Pseudocode would be,

```
Step  1:  Read N.
Step  2:  Initialize  power  to  1.
Step  3:  Repeat N times:
Step  4:           Double  power.
Step  5:  End  repeat
Step  6:  Write  power.
Step  7:  Stop.
```

1.9   BASIC CONCEPTS OF A C PROGRAM

This section describes main features of C like comments, header, general structure of C language is followed in every program.

Text opening with /* and ending with */ is treated as a comment and it will be ignored by the compiler. The comment can occur in any part of the program, and can extent to multiple lines. Comments do not nest in C; that is, by mistake placing a comment within a comment has inadvertent results. Similarly, if you start a comment but forget to end it, then compiler will throw an error. Comment is a optional part of the program. We can specify program related text/logic within a comment.

Example:

/*Comments in C are used to give small description of program, title of program or authors details etc.*/

/*Find GCD of 2 given number */

Header file contains predefined functions, which are necessary to run the current program. All header files should be incorporated explicitly before a *main()* function. In C, the *#include* preprocessor directive triggers the compiler to replace that line with the whole text or contents of the header file including input/output functions. The *include* directive allows libraries of the code to be developed which help to ensure that everybody uses the same version of a data or procedural code throughout a program. It is easy to cross-reference where the components are used in a system. It is easy to the change programs when needed because it has only one master copy to change and it saves time too.

Example: *#include<stdio.h>*

The body of C program is called as action or logic portion of the program. After header line, C program will be placed between opening brace({) and closing brace(}). All C program execution begins with *main()* function.

C program can contain functions which are building blocks of any big C programs. There is one mandatory function in C is called as *main()* function. C program will use set of built-in functions like *printf()*, *scanf()* etc..

C programs will have variables to hold the value like numbers, strings and complex data for manipulation. Similarly, Statements and Expressions are used in the body of program. Expressions contains variables and constants to evaluate a new values. And statements are nothing but expressions, assignments, function calls, or control flow statements.

Example:Below code is the basic structure of a C program.

```
#include <stdio.h>
main()
{/* start:body of program */
printf("Hello World");/* body of the program */
return 0;
}/* end:body of program */
```

The processing of source code of C files (.c) and creating an object file is called as *Compilation*, then creation of a single executable file from multiple object files is called as *Linking*. The *Loading* is the process where a program loads the executable file into the primary memory of the system.

1.10 DECLARATION, ASSIGNMENT AND PRINT STATEMENT

Declaration: Declaration specifies the storage location or variables to use in the C program. A variable in C is a name for a physical location within the system that can hold one value at a time. Every variable in C has a particular data type, which verifies the size and layout of the memory of variable; the range of data that can be stored within that memory; and the set of operations that can be applied to the variable. The name of a variable can be composed of letters, digits, and the underscore character. It must start with either a letter or an underscore. Upper and lower-case letters are different because C is case-sensitive.

A variable definition tells to the compiler where and how much to create the storage for the variable. A variable definition specifies a data type and contains a list of one or more variables of that type.

Syntax: data_type variable_list;

Here, *data_type* must be a valid C data type including *char, int, float, double* or any user-defined object, etc., and *variable_list* may consist of one or more identifier names separated by commas and ended by semicolon/punctuation(;).

Example:

int num, sqnum; / declares 2 variables as num, sqnum of int data type */*
*int num1; /*where, int is a data type, num1 is a variable name.*/*
int sqnum1;
char c;
float f=1.0;
*const double d=2.123456789; /*where const is a keyword, double is a data type ,d is a variable name, i.e the value of variable d is constant through out the program.*/*

Assignment Statement: Assignment statement is used to assign the value to the variable or sets and/or resets the data accumulated in the storage location(s) indicated by a variable name; that is, it copies the value into the variable. In an assignment statement, we use symbol '=' called assignment operator.

Syntax: *name of variable = value of expression;*

Example: *int num=4;*

This statement puts 4 into the storage location associated with the variable *num*. Assignment operator assigns values from right side operands to left side operand, in the above example, operator will assign value 4 into *num*.

Print Statement: The *printf* function is an output function, it is used for a formatted string to the *stdout* stream.

Syntax: printf("Control String", List of Variables or expressions to be displayed);

Control String describes the output as well as provides a placeholder to insert the formatted string. Format specifiers are used in the control string. Below are some format specifiers for particular data type,

int datatype: %d

float datatype: %f

char datatype: %c

Example:*printf("%d%d\n",num,sqnum);* Here *printf* will print/display *num* and *sqnum*, then move to new line(\n).

To print literal string, just place inside parentheses. The other form of *printf* is, print the value of one or more expressions.

Guidelines for *printf* statement:

(a) A *printf* is a powerful function for printing numbers, strings and other things stored in variables.

(b) In the most simple case, *printf* takes one argument: a string of characters to be printed.

(c) A *printf* contains a control string or format string in quotation marks. The control string not necessarily followed by some variables or expressions.

(d) Whenever we need to print a value, it requires conversion specification(e.g. %d)to hold its place in the control string. Here conversion specification describes the exact way the value is to be displayed and each conversion specification is replaced by the value of corresponding expression, then displayed according to the rules of specification.

(e) Use \n to print a newline(called as newline character and moves cursor to next line).

(f) If you include blank space, punctuation symbol etc. in the control string, it will print exactly as it appears.

(g) If you want to display values of expressions/variables, commas are used to separate each expression/variable from control string and each other, adding a blank space in between commas are immaterial because whatever expression occurs after the control string will be evaluated and then displayed based on its specification.

(h) If a control string has a single blank space between the two specifications, then output will contain a single blank space between the two values.

1.11   TYPES OF OPERATORS AND EXPRESSIONS

Operators are symbols which specifies what is to be done with variables and values. A variable's value keeps on changing throughout the program execution. Actually, data is not stored in the variable but points to a particular memory location. As we all know, data is stored in the memory of the computer. A variable is the name specified to the location of memory. A variable can be one of different data types.

Rules for constructing variable names:

(a) A variable name consists of any combination of digits, alphabets and underscores. Few compiler allows variable names whole length could be upto 247 *char*s. But it would be safer to bond to the ruling of 31 *char*s.

(b) The first character of the variable name must either be underscore or alphabet. It should not start with the digit.

(c) No commas and blanks are allowed in the variable name.

(d) No special symbols other than underscore(_) are allowed in the variable name.

(e) We need to declare the type of the variable name before making use of that name in the program.

Expressions: Combines variables and constants to evaluate new value.

Data Types and Size:

The C language provides 4 basic data types, they are *char, int, float, double* with optional specifiers (*signed, unsigned, short, long*). All data types are listed in the below table 1.2.

Type	Size and Explanation
char	A single byte which holds one character in the local character set.
int	Integer data type. Typically it is 16 bits in size.
float	Single precision floating-point type. Usually 32 bits in size.
double	Double precision floating-point type. Usually 64 bits in size.
signed char	Same size as char, but assured to be signed.
unsigned char	Same size as char, but assured to be unsigned.
short, short int, signed short, signed short int	short signed integer type. At least 16 bits in size.
unsigned short, unsigned short int	same as short, but unsigned.
signed int, unsigned, unsigned int	Basic signed/unsigned integer type. Typically it is 16 bits in size.
unsigned, unsigned int	Same as int, but unsigned.
long, long int, signed long, signed long int	long signed integer type. At least 32 bits in size.
unsigned long, unsigned long int	Same as long, but unsigned.
long long, long long int, signed long long, signed long long int	Long long signed integer type. At least 64 bits in size.
unsigned long long, unsigned long long int	Same as long long, but unsigned.
long double	Extended accuracy floating-point type.

Table 1.2 Data Types and its Size

Constants: Constants are also like regular variables, but, their values can not be modified by the program once they are defined. Constant refer to fixed or unchangeable value. They are also called as literals of the program. Constants can have any of the data type.

*Syntax: const data_type variable_name; (or) const data_type *variable_name;*

We can define constants in a C program by using *const* keyword and by using *#define* preprocessor directive, if we try to change constant values after defining in the C program, it will through an error. Below table 1.3 lists major types of constants and its rules.

Constant type	Data type	Example	Rules

Character constants	char	'X'	This constant is a single alphabet, a single digit or a single special symbol enclosed within single quotes. The maximum length of a character constant is 1 character.
Integer constants	int, unsigned int, long int, long long int	22, -11 for int. 123u for unsigned int. 1234 for long int.	The permissible range for integer constants is -32768 to 32767. This constant must have at least one digit and must not have a decimal point. This constant either be positive or negative. No commas or blanks are endorsed within an integer constant. If no sign heads an integer constant, it is assumed to be positive.
Floating point constants	float, double	22.123 for float, 900.123456789 for double	This constant must have at least one digit and can have a decimal point. Real value could be either positive or negative. No commas or blanks are endorsed within an float constant. If no sign heads an float constant, it is assumed to be positive.
Octal constant	int	012	Octal starts with 0.
Hexadecimal constant	int	0X70	Hexa starts with 0X.
String constants	char	"BC"	String constants are enclosed within double quotes.

Table 1.3 Constant Types and its Rules

As you know, ♯*define* is used to define a constant and this constant is used across a C program. Example: ♯*define SIZE 100 /* using preprocessor directive*/

Backslash Character Constants:

In C, there are some characters which have special meaning and they should be preceded by backslash symbol to make use of special function of them. Table 1.4 lists the Backslash Character Constants.

Backslash Character	Meaning

\a	Alert or bell
\b	Backspace
\f	Form feed
\n	New line
\r	Carriage return
\t	Horizontal tab
\v	Vertical tab
\\	Backslash
\?	Question mark
\'	Single quote
\"	Double quote
\ooo	Octal number
\xhh	Hexadecimal number

Table 1.4 Backslash Character Constants

Arithmetic Operators: These Operators are used to perform Arithmetic Operations. Table 1.5 lists all Arithmetic Operators.

Operator	Description	Example
+	Adds two operands.	A + B
-	Subtracts second operand from the first.	A - B
*	Multiply both operands.	A * B
/	Divide numerator by denumerator.	B / A
%	Modulus Operator and remainder of an integer division.	B % A
++	Increment operator, increases integer value by 1.	A++
- -	Decrement operator, decreases integer value by one.	A- -

Table 1.5 Arithmetic Operators

Relational Operators: Relational Operators are used to test or define some kind of relation(compare) between two entities. Table 1.6 lists all relational operators. Assuming A=5 and B=10.

Operator	Description	Example
==	Checks if the values of two operands are equal or not, if yes then condition becomes true.	(A == B) is not true.
! =	Checks if the values of two operands are equal or not, if values are not identical then condition turns into true.	(A ! = B) is true.
>	Verifies if the value of left operand is bigger than the value of right operand, if yes then condition turns into true.	(A >B) is not true.
<	Verifies if the value of left operand is smaller than the value of right operand, if yes then condition turns into true.	(A < B) is true.

>=	Verifies if the value of left operand is bigger than or equal to the value of right operand, if yes then condition becomes true.	(A >= B) is not true.
<=	Verifies if the value of left operand is smaller than or equal to the value of right operand, if yes then condition becomes true.	(A <= B) is true.

Table 1.6 Relational Operators

Logical Operators: Logical operators evaluate expressions and decide what boolean should be expressed from the evaluation. A logical operator combines one or two conditions into a single new condition. Below table 1.7 lists all logical operators. Assuming A=1 and B=0.

Operator	Description	Example
&&	Called Logical AND operator. If both the operands are non-zero, then condition becomes true.	(A && B) is false.
||	Called Logical OR Operator. If any of the two operands is non-zero, then condition becomes true.	(A || B) is true.
!	Called Logical NOT Operator. Use to reverses the logical state of its operand. If a condition is true then Logical NOT operator will make it false.	!(A&&B) is true.

Table 1.7 Logical Operators

Type Conversion:

Type Conversion (casting) is used to convert a variable from one data type to another data type.

Example: let us assume that, store a *long* value into a simple integer then you can type cast *long* to *int*. You can achieve this kind of conversion using the cast operator.

There are 2 kinds of conversions: implicit casting and explicit casting.

Implicit Type Conversion:

When the type translation is carried out automatically by the compiler without programmers involvement, such type of translation is known as implicit type conversion or type promotion. The rules of evaluating expressions are given below:

All *short* and *char* are involuntarily transformed to *int*.

If any of the operand is of type *long double*, then others will be transformed to *long double* and result will be *long double*. Or, if any of the operand is *double*, then others are changed to *double*. Or, if any of the operand is *float*, then others are converted to *float*. Or, if any of the operand is *unsigned long int*, then others will be converted to *unsigned long int*. Or, if any operand is *long int* then other will be converted to *long int*. Or, if any operand is *unsigned int* then others will be converted to *unsigned int*.

Conversion of *float* to *int* causes truncation of fractional part, translation of *double* to *float* makes rounding of digits and the translation of *long int* to *int* causes dropping of excess upper order bits.

Note: The final result of expression is converted to type of variable on left side of assignment operator before assigning value to it.

Explicit Type Conversion:

The type translation carried out by the programmer by enforcing the data type of the expression of specific type is called as type casting.

Syntax: *(data_type)expression;*

where, *data_type* is any valid C data type, and expression may be constant, variable or expression.

Example: x=(int)a+b*d;

Certain rules have to be followed while converting the expression from one type to another to avoid the loss of data and they are,

a. All *int* types to be converted to *float*.

b. All *float* types to be converted to *double*.

c. All *char* types to be converted to *int*.

Example: Below code snippet will show the type conversion,

```
#include <stdio.h>
main()
{
        int i=10;
        float f;
        char c;
        c='A';
        f=(float)i/3;
        double d;
        printf("i=%d and f=%f \n", i,f );
        d=(double)f*8;
        i=c;
        printf("d=%f and i = %d",d,i );
}
```

Output:

i=10 and f=3.333333

d=26.666666 and i=65

Increment and Decrement Operators:

Increment or decrement operators are unary operators that add or subtract one from their operand respectively.

Increment operators (++):

Increment operators are used to increase the value of subsequent. Value may be increased according to the programmer specification. Increment operator are two types as follows :

Assume i=5.

a. Post increment, e.g. i++; increments *i* after its has been used, hence value of *i*(5) is first used and later moved to 6.

b. Pre increment, e.g. ++i; increment *i* before its value is used, hence value of *i* is moved to 6 before it is used.

Decrement operators (--):

Decrement operators are used to decrease the value to one, two and so on. As like increment operators, decrement operators are also two type as follows:

a. Post decrement, e.g. i--; decrements *i* after its has been used, hence value of *i*(5) is first used and later moved to 4.

b. Pre decrement, e.g. --i; decrement *i* before its value is used, hence the value of *i* is moved to 4 before it is used.

Bitwise Operators:

A bitwise function operates on one or more bit patterns or binary numerals at the level of their individual bits. Bitwise operators are listed in table 1.8.

Symbol	Operator	Example
&	bitwise AND	a=0,b=0; $a\&b \Rightarrow 0$ a=0,b=1; $a\&b \Rightarrow 0$ a=1,b=0; $a\&b \Rightarrow 0$ a=1,b=1; $a\&b \Rightarrow 1$
|	bitwise inclusive OR	a=0,b=0; $a|b \Rightarrow 0$ a=0,b=1; $a|b \Rightarrow 1$ a=1,b=0; $a|b \Rightarrow 1$ a=1,b=1; $a|b \Rightarrow 1$(0 with carry 1)
∧	bitwise exclusive OR(XOR)	a=0,b=0; $a \wedge b \Rightarrow 0$ a=0,b=1; $a \wedge b \Rightarrow 1$ a=1,b=0; $a \wedge b \Rightarrow 1$ a=1,b=1; $a \wedge b \Rightarrow 0$
<<	left shift	i=14; j=i $<< 1$; Output: Bit pattern for 14 is 1110, move 1 bit left, so it will be 11100 which is 28 in decimal.
>>	right shift	i=14; j=i $>> 1$; Output: Bit pattern for 14 is 1110, move 1 bit right, so it will be 111 which is 7 in decimal.
⁓	bitwise NOT (one's complement) (unary)	a=0; $⁓ a \Rightarrow 1$ a=1; $⁓ a \Rightarrow 0$

Table 1.8 Bitwise Operators

Assignment Operators:

An assignment operation assigns the value of right-hand operand to the storage location named by the left-hand operand. Hence, the left-hand operand of an assignment operation must be a modifiable l-value otherwise you get compiler error. After the assignment, an assignment expression has the value of the left operand but it is not an l-value. The left operand must not be an array, function, constant. The assignment operators can both transform and assign values in a single operation, assignment operators are listed in table 1.9.

Operator	Operation Performed	Example
=	Simple assignment	a=2;
*=	Multiplication assignment	a*=b;
/=	Division assignment	a/=b;
%=	Remainder assignment	a%=b;
+=	Addition assignment	a+=b;
− =	Subtraction assignment	a- =b;
<<=	Left-shift assignment	a<<=b;

>>=	Right-shift assignment	a>>=b;
& =	Bitwise-AND assignment	a& =b;
∧=	Bitwise-exclusive-OR assignment	a∧=b;
|=	Bitwise-inclusive-OR assignment	a|=b;

Table 1.9 Assignment Operators

Conditional Expressions:

The conditional operator in C is also known as ternary operator(?:). This operator takes three arguments hence called as Ternary operator. The conditional operator evaluates an expression returning a value if that condition is not *false* and different one if the expression is evaluated as *false*.
Syntax: expr1 ? expr2 : expr3;
If the expr1(condition) is true, expr2 is returned else expr3 is returned.
Example:*z =(a>b)?a:b;* say, a=10, b=20, then z will have 20.

Precedence and Order of Evaluation:

Operator precedence resolves which operator will be performed first in a group of operators with different precedences. For instance 4 + 3 * 2 is calculated as 4 + (3 * 2), giving 10, and not as (4 + 3) * 2, giving 14 which is wrong.
The operator associativity rules describe the order in which adjacent operators with the same precedence level are calculated. For example, the expression 7 - 3 - 2 is calculated as (7 - 3) - 2, giving 2, and and not as 7 - (3 - 2), giving 6. In this case we say that subtraction is left associative meaning that the left most subtraction must be done first. Operator precedence and order of evaluation is listed in table 1.10.

Operator Name	Associativity	Operators
Primary	left to right	() [ ] . – >
Unary	right to left	++ -- + – ! ∽ & * (type_name)
Multiplicative	left to right	* / %
Additive	left to right	+ -
Bitwise Shift	left to right	<< >>
Relational	left to right	< > <= >=
Equality	left to right	== !=
Bitwise AND	left to right	&
Bitwise Exclusive OR	left to right	∧
Bitwise Inclusive OR	left to right	|
Logical AND	left to right	&&
Logical OR	left to right	||
Conditional	right to left	? :
Assignment	right to left	= += – = *= / = <<= >>= %= &= ∧= |=
Comma	left to right	,

Table 1.10 Precedence and Associativity Operators

Chapter 2

BRANCHING and LOOPING

In this chapter the order of execution of the statements of program is described. A statement is terminated with semicolon. Braces { and } are used to group the statements together into a *compound statement* known as **block**. The order of executing the individual statements is known as *control flow* (or alternatively, flow of control) or *program flow*. Generally, the statements of program are executed in the same order as it appears in the program. Such execution is known as *sequential execution*. However, the order of execution of the statements or **control flow** can be varied using *Branching* and *Looping*. Where, branching is used to decide which section of code to be executed based on the condition being either *True* or *False*. Looping is used to execute certain sections of code multiple times based on the condition being *True* or *False*. The statements which change the execution of statements from sequential to non-sequential are known as control statements.

2.1 TWO-WAY SELECTION

In this section, control statements which are used to execute the one of sections based on the condition are described. However, the result of the condition is either *True* or *False*. If result of the condition of is *True* one section is executed. Otherwise, alternate section of the program is executed. Following two-way branching statements are discussed

- *if* statement

- *if-else* statement

- Nested *if-else* statement

- Cascaded *if-else* statement

- *switch* statement

- Ternary operator

2.1.1 *if* statement

if statement is used to executes single statement or block, if the condition result is *true*. Otherwise the statement following the single or compound statement are ignored. The flow chart illustrating the flow of control using *if* statement is given in Fig 2.1. The syntax of the *if* statement is as follows

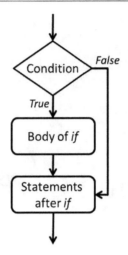

Figure 2.1 Flow chart illustrating the flow of control using *if* statement

Syntax:
```
if( condition )
{
block 1;
}
```

where, *if* is the keyword, *condition* is the logical statement and *block* within the { and } are multiple statements to be executed.

Example: If *N* is an integer, determine *N* is positive?

```c
#include <stdio.h>
main()
{
int N = 10;
if(N >= 0) {
printf("N is a positive number");
}
}
```
Output:
```
10 is a positive number
```

In the above program, the value of the variable *N* is *10*, which is positive. Hence the output. Rather than writing the code after *if* statement as *block*, it can also be written as single statement as follows

```c
#include <stdio.h>
main()
{
int N = 10;
if(N >= 0)
printf("N is a positive number");
}
```
Output:
```
10 is a positive number
```

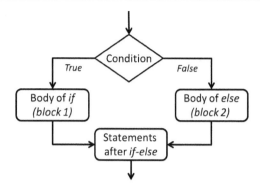

Figure 2.2 Flow chart illustrating the control flow for *if-else* statement

2.1.2 *if-else* statement

if statement is used to executes single statement or block of code, if the result of the condition is *true*. If there is a need to execute some other statement or block of code if the condition is *false*, *if-else* statement is used. The flow chart illustrating the control flow for *if-else* statement is given in Fig 2.2. The syntax of the *if-else* statement is as follows

```
Syntax:
if( condition )
{
block 1;
}
else
{
block 2;
}
```

where, *if* and *else* are the keywords, *condition* is the logical statement, and the *block 1* and *block 2* within the { and } are to be statements to be executed if the *condition* result is *True* and *False* respectively.

Example: If *N* is an integer, determine *N* is positive or negative?

```
#include <stdio.h>
main()
{
int N = -10;
if(N >= 0) {
printf("N is a positive number",N);
}
else
{
printf("N is a negative number",N);
}


}
Output:
-10 is a negative number
```

In the above program, the value of the variable *N* is *-10*, which is negative. Hence the output. The code after *if* and *else* statements can be written as single statement as follows

```
#include <stdio.h>
main()
{
int N = -10;
if(N >= 0)
printf("N is a positive number",N);
else
printf("N is a negative number",N);
}
Output:
-10 is a negative number
```

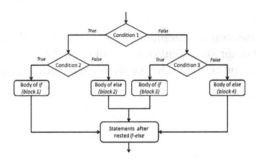

Figure 2.3 Flow chart illustrating the control flow for nested *if-else* statement

2.1.3   Nested *if-else* statement

The *if-else* statement allows a choice to be made between two possible alternatives. However, sometimes there is need to make choice between more than two possibilities. The, *if-else* statement places within another *if-else* for making further choices is known as nested *if-else* statements. The flow chart illustrating the control flow for nested *if-else* statement is given in Fig 2.3. The syntax of the nested *if-else* statement is as follows

```
Syntax:
if( condition 1)
{
if( condition 2)
{
block 1;
}
else
{
block 2;
}

}
else
{
```

```
if( condition 3)
{
block 3;
}
else
{
block 4;
}

}
```

where, *if* and *else* are the keywords, *condition 1, condition 2* and *condition 3* are the logical statement. The execution of *block 1, block 2, block 3* and *block 4* are executed based on the results of the conditions as given in Table 2.1.3.

	Condition 2		Condition 3	
	True	False	True	False
Condition 1: True	Block 1	Block 2	–	–
Condition 1: False	–	–	Block 3	Block 4

Example: Given three integers *a*, *b* and *c*, find the greatest of all these values ?

```
#include <stdio.h>
main()
{
int a = -10, b = 9, c = 35;
if(a > b) {
if(a > c)
printf("%d is greatest",a);
else
printf("%d is greatest",c);

}
else
{
if(b > c)
printf("%d is greatest",b);
else
printf("%d is greatest",c);
}


}
Output:
35 is greatest
```

In the above program, the value of the variable *c* is *35*, which is greater than *a = -10* and *b = 9*. Hence the output.

2.1.4 Cascaded *if-else* statement

A form of *if-else* statement in which each *else* block (except the last) consists of a further nested *if-else* blocks is known cascaded *if-else* statement. It is used when a set of test conditions are to be performed

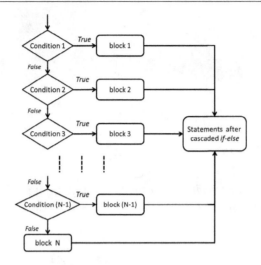

Figure 2.4 Flow chart illustrating the control flow for cascaded *if-else* statement

serially or hierarchically. The *if* statements are executed serially until any of the *condition* is *True* or ends up arriving at else block. The flow chart illustrating the control flow for cascaded *if-else* statement is given in Fig 2.4. The syntax of the *if-else* statement is as follows

```
Syntax:
if( condition 1)
{
block 1;
}
else if( condition 2)
{
block 2;
}
else if( condition 2)
{
block 3;
}
.
.
.
else
{
block N;
}
```

where, *if* and *else* are the keywords. *condition 1*, *condition 2* and *condition N* are the logical statements. The conditions are evaluated serially, and the block associated with condition which is *True* is executed. The remaining *blocks* and associated *conditions* are not executed. If none of the *if conditions* are *True*, the *block N* associated with the last *else* is executed. Cascaded *if-else* gives provided more readability.

   Example: Write a program which receives your marks and then determine the class.

```
#include <stdio.h>
main()
```

```
{
int N;

printf("Enter your marks between 0 and 100:");
scanf("%d",&N);
if(N >= 70)
printf("\n %d marks is First class with distinction",N);
else if(N >= 60)
printf("\n %d marks is First class",N);
else if(N >= 50)
printf("\n %d marks is Second class",N);
else if(N >= 35)
printf("\n %d marks is pass class ",N);
else
printf("\n %d marks is fail",N);

}
Output:
Run 1
Enter your marks between 0 and 100: 75
75 marks is First class with distinction

Run 2
Enter your marks between 0 and 100: 65
65 marks is First class
```

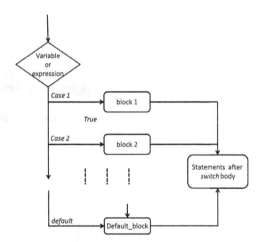

Figure 2.5 Flow chart illustrating the control flow for *switch* statement

2.2   *SWITCH* STATEMENT

Similar to *if-else*, *switch* provides multiple choice branching. This is suitable where several choices are required. Block corresponding to matching case is executed. The flow chart illustrating the control flow for *switch* statement is given in Fig 2.5. The syntax of the *switch* statement is as follows

```
Syntax:
switch(variable)
{
case 1: block 1
break;

case 2: block 2
break;

case 3: block 3
break;
.
.
.

case N: block N
break;

default: Default_block
}
```

switch, case, default and *break* are keywords. The body of a *switch* statement is known as a *switch* block. A statements between the braces { and } is the *switch* block it can have one or more *case*. However, *default* label is optional. The *switch* statement evaluates its expression, then the control is transferred to the matching case label. The corresponding block is executed until *break* statement is encountered. If the variable does not match to any of the mentioned *case*s, then Default_block is executed. Further, it can be noted that there does not exists break statement at the end of default_block. default_block Further, it can be noted that there does not exists break statement at the end of default_block.

In *if-else*, tests for the conditions based on ranges of values, such as ($a >= b$) or ($a < b$), etc. But, the *switch* statement tests *variable* based only on a single integer value or constant only. That is you can have *case* value such as ($a < b$). *switch* is a multi-way branching. *switch* is faster than *if-else* because only one variable is tested. In case of *if-else* more than one condition is tested.

Example: Write a program which receives the number representing the weekday and displays the name of the corresponding weekday.

```
#include<stdio.h>
main()
{
int N;

printf("Enter the number of weekday:");
scanf("%d",&N);

switch(N)
{
case 1: printf("Sunday\n");
break;

case 2: printf("Monday\n");
break;
```

```
case 3: printf("Tuesday\n");
break;

case 4: printf("Wednesday\n");
break;

case 5: printf("Thursday\n");
break;

case 6: printf("Friday\n");
break;

case 7: printf("Saturday\n");
break;

default: printf("Wrong input\n");

}
```

```
Output:

Run 1
Enter the number of weekday: 2
Monday

Run 2
Enter the number of weekday: 7
Saturday

Run 3
Enter the number of weekday: 10
Wrong input
```

2.3 TERNARY OPERATOR

The ternary operator is similar to the way *if-else* conditional expression. The syntax of ternary operator is as follows

```
condition ? statement 1: statement 2;
```

where *condition* is a expression which results in boolean value. *statement 1* is returned if the boolean *condition* produces *True*. Otherwise, *statement 2* is returned.

Example: Write a program to find the greater of two numbers using ternary operator.

```
#include<stdio.h>
main()
{
int A, B, Res;
```

```
printf("Enter two numbers:");
scanf("%d%d",&A, &B);

Res = (A > B) ? A : B;

printf(" %d is greater\n", Res);
}
```

Output:

```
Run 1
Enter two numbers: 4 26
26 is greater

Run 2
Enter two numbers: 14 6
14 is greater
```

Example: Write a program to receive a number from user and then print the absolute value of the same.

```
#include<stdio.h>
main()
{
int N, Res;

printf("Enter a number:");
scanf("%d",&N);

Res = (N > 0) ? N : -N;

printf(" Absolute value of %d is %d \n", N, Res);
}
```

Output:

```
Run 1
Enter a number: -4
Absolute value of -4 is 4

Run 2
Enter two numbers: 20
Absolute value of 20 is 20
```

2.4 LOOPS

Sometimes, there is need to execute the certain block of code repeatedly until test *condition* is *true*. This can be achieved using loops. However, as soon is *condition* becomes *false*, control flow branches outside the loop. Each round of the loop is also known as *iteration*. C language provides three different kinds of loops known as (i) **for**, (ii) **while** and (iii) **do-while**.

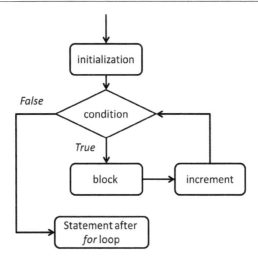

Figure 2.6 Flow chart illustrating the control flow of *for* statement

2.4.1 for-loop

A *for* loop is a control statement which executes block until condition is *true*. The repeated execution of the block is called as iterations. The syntax of the for loop is as follows:

```
for(initialization ; condition ; increment)
{
block
}
```

where *for* is a keyword. *initialization* is assignment expression where variables are initialized, and *increment* is a expression where variables values are updated for each iteration. The initialization statement is executed only once at the beginning of the *for* loop. Then, the test *condition* is verified by the program. If the test *condition* is *false*, *for* loop is terminated. If the test *condition* is *true* then the block inside body of *for* loop is executed and then update expression is updated. This process repeats until test *condition* is *false*. The flowchart of *for* is illustrated in Fig 2.6. However, *initialization*, *condition* and *increment* are optional. By default, *condition* is always *true*. It can be given as follows

```
for( ; ; )
{
block
}
```

Example: Write a program to obtain a number N from the user and display all the odd numbers less than N. *Hint*: Odd number is not divisible by 2.

```
#include<stdio.h>
main()
{
int N, i;

printf("Enter a number:");
scanf("%d",&N);
```

```
for (i = 1; i<=N ; i++)
{
Res = i % 2;

if( Res > 0) /* odd number is not divisible by 2 */
printf("%d \t",i);
}


}

Output:

Run 1
Enter a numbers: 6
1 3 5

Run 2
Enter two numbers: 11
1 3 5 7 9 11
```

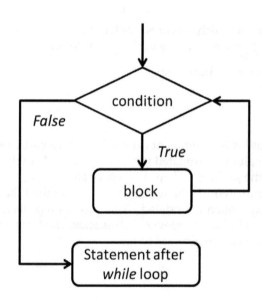

Figure 2.7 Flow chart illustrating the control flow of *while* statement

2.4.2   while-statement

while statement is similar to *for* loop, executes the block of code until the boolean condition results is *true*. But, while does not have *initialization* expression and *increment*. The flow chart illustrating the *while* loop is shown in Fig 2.7. The syntax of the *while* loop is as follows:

```
while( condition )
{
block
```

```
}
```

where *while* is a keyword and code block inside the braces { and } is its body. The *while* loop checks whether the test condition is *true*. If it is *true*, code block inside the braces { and } is executed. Then for the next iteration, the test condition is verified for *true*. This process continues until the test condition becomes *false*. Example: Write a program to display the factorial of the number provided by user. *Hint*: Factorial of $N = 1 \times 2 \times \cdots N$

```c
#include<stdio.h>
main()
{
int N, Fact = 1;

printf("Enter a number:");
scanf("%d",&N);

while( N >= 1)
{
Fact =  Fact * N;
N = N - 1;
}

printf("Factorial of %d is %d \n",N, Fact);

}

Output:

Run 1
Enter a number: 3
Factorial of 3 is 6

Run 1
Enter a number: 5
Factorial of 5 is 120
```

2.4.3 do-while statement

do-while loop is similar to *while* loop. It executes the block of code until the condition is true. Unlike to *for* loop, it does not have *initialization* and *updating* expressions. The flow chart for do-while loop is illustrated in the Fig 2.8. The syntax of the *do-while* loop is as follows

```c
do
{
block
}while( condition );
```

where *do* and *while* are the keywords, and *block* is the code that is executed until the boolean *condition* is *true*. The *block* code is the body of *do-while*. The primary difference between *while* and *do-while* is that, in case of *do-while* the boolean *condition* is evaluated after executing the *block*. But, in case of *while* the boolean *condition* is evaluated before executing the *block*. So, the block is executed at least once in *do-while* loops. Example: Write a C program to add all the numbers entered by a user until user enters 0.

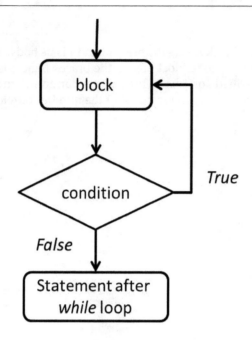

Figure 2.8 Flow chart illustrating the control flow of *do-while* statement

```
#include<stdio.h>

main()
{
int num, sum = 0;

do
{
printf("Enter a number:");
scanf("%d",&num);

sum = sum + num;

}while( num != 0 )

printf("\nSum of the numbers provided by user is %d", sum);

}


Output:

Enter a number: 3
Enter a number: 6
Enter a number: -5
Enter a number: 12
Enter a number: 0
```

```
Sum of the numbers provided by user is 16
```

2.5 JUMP STATEMENTS

Jump statements move the control to some other section of the program. These are also called as branching statements. Further these statement move the control without any boolean condition. Thus, they are known as unconditional control statements. There are three types of jumps statements as follows

- *goto*

- *continue*

- *break*

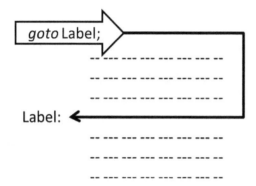

Figure 2.9 Flow chart of *goto* statement with *label* appearing later

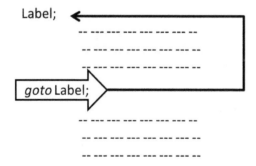

Figure 2.10 Flow chart of *goto* statement with *label* appearing before

2.5.1 *goto*-statement

It is used for transferring the control to some other *label* or *tag* location of the program. The syntax of *goto* is as follows

```
goto label;
```

where *goto* is the keyword. *label* is the identifier. When the control reaches *goto*, it is moved to the identifier and the code execution resumes from there. The label or identifier can occur after or before *goto*. The illustration of *goto* is given in Fig 2.9. It can be observed in 2.10 and 2.9, that the label or identifier appears before and after *goto* statement respectively.

Example: Write a C program to receive the numbers from user and display the same until user provides negative number.

```c
#include<stdio.h>

main()
{
int num, count = 0;

Here:
printf("Enter a number:");
scanf("%d",&num);


if(num >= 0 )
{
   count = count + 1;
goto Here;
}

printf("\nPositive numbers provided by user are %d", count);

}
```

```
Output:
Run 1
Enter a number: 3
Enter a number: 6
Enter a number: -5

Positive numbers provided by user are 2


Run 2
Enter a number: 76
Enter a number: 2
Enter a number: 4
Enter a number: 8
Enter a number: 22
Enter a number: 39
Enter a number: -14

Positive numbers provided by user are 6
```

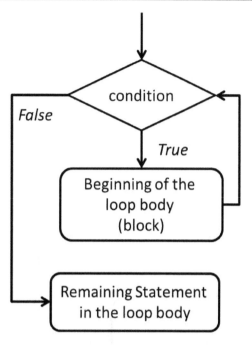

Figure 2.11 Flow chart of *continue* statement

2.5.2   continue

continue statement is used to skip the following statements inside the loop and the control is moved to the beginning of the loop. Further, the control does not go out of the loop. *continue* is always used inside the loop. Flow chart of *continue* is shown in Fig 2.11. The syntax of *continue* is as follows

```
continue;
```

Example: Write a program to receive a numbers N and D from user and display all the numbers from 1 to N which are not divisible by D. Hint: if $N = 5$ and $D = 3$, then $1, 2, 4$.

```c
#include<stdio.h>

main()
{
int N, D, i, res;

printf("Enter N:");
scanf("%d",&N);

printf("Enter D:");
scanf("%d",&D);

for (i = 1 ; i <= N ; i++)
{
res = i%D; /* if i is divisible by D then reminder is zero */

if(res == 0)
```

```
continue;

printf("%d,\t", i);
}
}
```

```
Output:
Run 1
Enter N: 10
Enter D: 2
1, 3, 5, 7, 9

Run 2
Enter N: 9
Enter D: 3
1, 2, 4, 5, 7, 8
```

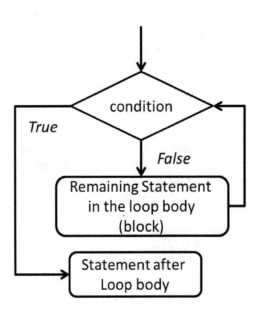

Figure 2.12 Flow chart of *break* statement

2.5.3   break-statement

break statement is used for terminating the loop or terminate out of *switch*. When used inside any of loops, the statements after *break* statement are omitted and the control moves out to end of the loop body. Similarly, when *break* is used in *switch*, the control is moved out of *switch* body. Flow chart of *break* statement is shown in Fig 2.12. The syntax for *break* statement is as follows

```
break;
```

Example: Write a program to receive a numbers *N* and *D* from user and display all the numbers from 1 to *N* which are less than *D* only.

```
#include<stdio.h>

main()
{
int N, D;

printf("Enter N:");
scanf("%d",&N);

printf("Enter D:");
scanf("%d",&D);

for (i = 1 ; i <= N ; i++)
{
if(i >= D)
break;

printf("%d,\t", i);
}
}
```

```
Output:
Run 1
Enter N: 10
Enter D: 7
1, 2, 3, 4, 5, 6

Run 2
Enter N: 5
Enter D: 13
1, 2, 3, 4, 5
```

2.6 EXAMPLE PROGRAMS

Write a program to determine whether the person is senior citizen or not.

```
#include <stdio.h>

main()
{
int Age;

printf("Enter the age of the person:");
scanf("%d",&d);

if( Age >= 60)
printf(" Yes, senior citizen");
```

```
else
printf(" Not a senior citizen");


}
```

Output:

```
Run 1:
Enter the age of the person: 73
Yes, senior citizen

Run 2:
Enter the age of the person: 25
Not a senior citizen
```

Example: Write a C program to determine whether the year provided by user is leap year using cascading *if* statement ?

```
#include <stdio.h>

main()
{
  int Year, Res;

  printf("Enter a year :");
  scanf("%d", &Year);

  if ( Year%400 == 0)
    printf("%d : Leap year", Year);
  else if ( Year%100 == 0)
    printf("%d : Not a leap year", Year);
  else if ( Year%4 == 0 )
    printf("%d : Leap year", Year);
  else
    printf("%d : Not a leap year", Year);

}
```

Output:

```
Run 1:
Enter a year :  1992
1992 : Leap year

Run 2:
Enter a year :  1900
1992 : Not a leap year
```

Write a C program to print all the natural numbers upto N and are not divisible by divisor d provided by user.

```c
#include <stdio.h>

main()
{
  int MaxNum, Divisor;
  int i;

  printf("Enter the maximum limit :");
  scanf("%d", &MaxNum);

  printf("Enter the divisor :");
  scanf("%d", &Divisor);

for (i = 1; i <= MaxNum ; i++)
{

if (i % Divisor)
continue

printf("%d\t",i);
}
}
```

Output:

Run 1:
Enter the maximum limit: 20
Enter the divisor: 2
1 3 5 7 9 11 13 15 17 18 19

Run 1:
Enter the maximum limit: 10
Enter the divisor: 4
1 2 3 5 6 7 9 10

Example: Write a program to print the natural numbers equal to the rank of the row as follows

```
1
1 2
1 2 3
1 2 3 4
```

```c
#include <stdio.h>

main()
{
```

```
  int MaxRow;
  int i,j;

  printf("Enter the maximum row :");
  scanf("%d", &MaxRow);

for (i = 1; i <= MaxRow ; i++)
{
for (j = 1; j <= i ; j++)
printf("%d ",j);

printf("\n");
}
}
```

Example: Write a program to print all the numbers starting from a until its sum is less than the user provided limit L.

```
#include <stdio.h>

main()
{
  int Limit, a, sum = 0;
  int i,j;

  printf("Enter the initial number :");
  scanf("%d", &a);

  printf("Enter the limit :");
  scanf("%d", &Limit);

i = a;

while(1)
{
Limit += i;

if (sum > Limit )
break;

printf("%d ",i);

i = i + 1;
}
}
```

Output:

```
Run 1:
Enter the initial number : 3
```

```
Enter the limit : 10
3 4

Run 2:
Enter the initial number : 8
Enter the limit : 30
8 9 10
```

Chapter 3

ARRAYS

In the previous chapters declaring a variable and modify the value of the variable is discussed. However, assume a situation where there is a need to store the marks of 100 students of a class. If one variable is declared per student, 100 variables need to be declared. That is, declaring individual variables, such as *Stud*00, *Stud*01, $\cdots$, *Stud*99. Further, coding with correct use of variable name becomes extremely tedious. These type of problems can be handled in C programming using arrays.

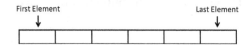

Figure 3.1 Illustrating of elements storing in array

Array is a data structure which can store elements of the same data type. Arrays can be of any data type such as **int, float, char** or **double**. Array is as a group of elements or variables that share a common name and each is defined by atleast one index or position. The elements are stored in continuous memory locations. The first element is stored in first address and last element is stored in the last address of the array variable as illustrated in the Fig 3.1. The syntax for declaring a array is as follows:

```
type ArrayVariableName [ arraySize ];
```

where, *type* is valid C language data type, *ArrayVariableName* is array identifier variable name and *arraySize* inside the braces [and] is an integer constant greater than zero which defines the size of array. Finally, declaration is terminated with semicolon. Arrays are of two types:

- One-dimensional array

- Multidimensional array

3.1   ONE-DIMENSIONAL ARRAY

One dimensional array is also known as single dimensional array. It is basically a linear list of memory locations used to store data. The syntax for declaring a one dimensional array is as follows:

Syntax:

```
<data-type> <array_name> [size];
```

where, *data-type* is valid C language data type, *ArrayVariableName* is array identifier variable name and *arraySize* inside the braces [and] is an integer constant greater than zero which defines the size of array. All the values or memory locations are accessed using same name and a one *index* or *subscript*. Example: Declaring two 5 element arrays with array names (i) *marks* of type *int* and (ii) *Weight* of type *float* are as follows,

```
int marks[5];
int Weight[5];
```

The one dimensional arrays can be initialized after declaration as follows

```
int marks[5] = {65, 80, 76, 70, 50, 35};
```

The number of comma separated values between braces { and } can not be larger than the array size that is declared between square brackets [and]. However, if the size of the array is omitted, the compiler assigns the array name or identifier with memory to hold the initialization. Therefore, if you write:

```
int marks[] = {65, 80, 76, 70, 50, 35};
```

marks array is assigned with 6 contiguous memory locations and initialized with $65, 80, 76, 70, 50$ and 35 as illustrated in Fig 3.2.

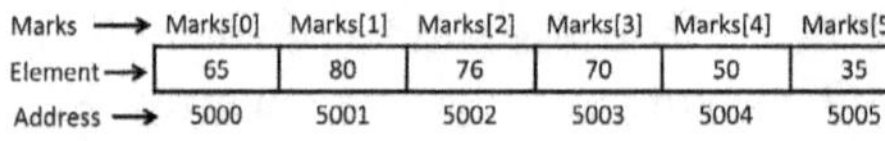

Marks →	Marks[0]	Marks[1]	Marks[2]	Marks[3]	Marks[4]	Marks[5]
Element →	65	80	76	70	50	35
Address →	5000	5001	5002	5003	5004	5005

Figure 3.2 Illustrating of elements and their address in one dimensional array

The individual element of one dimensional array are accessed by an index or subscript that is non negative integer. The first element of arrays have 0 as the index, which is also called base index and the last element index is total size of the array minus 1. An example for accessing a element of one dimensional arrays is as follows,

```
Result = marks[5];
```

The above statement will provide 5 element from the array *marks* and assign the value to *Result* variable. Graphical illustration of one dimensional arrays is given in Fig 3.2. Example: write a program to receive the marks of each subject and print the total sum.

```
#include<stdio.h>

main()
{
```

```
int marks[10];
int i = 0, Result = 0;

/* Receive marks from user and store it in array */
for (i = 0; i < 10; i++)
{
printf("Marks of subject %d", i);
scanf("%d", &marks[i]);
}

/* Compute sum of the marks from array */
for (i = 0; i < 10; i++)
{
Result = Result + marks [i];
}

printf("Total marks is: %d",Result);

}
```

Output:

```
Marks of subject 0: 65
Marks of subject 1: 80
Marks of subject 2: 76
Marks of subject 3: 70
Marks of subject 4: 50
```

Total marks is: 341

Write a C program to receive the marks of all the students from the user into a array, and then determine the maximum marks in the array.

```
#include<stdio.h>

main()
{
int Marks[100];
int N, MaxMarks, Temp;

printf("Enter the number of students (less than 100):");
scanf("%d", &N);

/* Receive the marks from the user and store it in array */
for (i = 0; i < N; i++)
{
printf("Marks of student %d", i+1);
```

```
scanf("%d", &Marks[i]);
}

/* Determine the maximum marks from array */
MaxMarks = Marks[0];
for (i = 0; i < N; i++)
{
if ( MaxMarks < marks [i])
MaxMarks = marks [i];
}

printf("\nMaximum marks is %d ",MaxMarks);

}
```

Output:

```
Enter the number of students (less than 100): 10
Marks of student 1: 15
Marks of student 2: 87
Marks of student 3: 45
Marks of student 4: 34
Marks of student 5: 96
Marks of student 6: 35
Marks of student 7: 63
Marks of student 8: 57
Marks of student 9: 97
Marks of student 10: 50

Maximum marks is 97
```

3.2   MULTIDIMENSIONAL ARRAY

Multidimensional array basically a non-linear list of memory locations used to store data. The dimension of the array can be determined by number of indexes required to access the individual element. Thus, we can have arrays of two-dimensional (2D), three dimensional (3D) and so on. The general form syntax for declaring a multidimensional dimensional array is as follows:

Syntax:

```
<data-type> <array_name> [size1][size2]...[sizeN];
```

where, *data-type* is the data type supported by C language, *array_name* is the identifier or array name and *size1*, *size2* and *sizeN* are size of the each dimension or index or subscript. Some examples of declaring a multidimensional array are as follows.

Syntax:

```
int Marks[10]; -> One dimensional array
```

```
int Matrix[2][3]; -> Two dimensional array
int Time[24][60][60]; -> Three dimensional array
```

where, *Marks*, *Matrix* and *Time* are one dimensional, two dimensional and three dimensional arrays respectively.

3.2.1 Two-dimensional arrays:

Two two-dimensional array is the simplest form of the multidimensional array. For easy understanding, a two-dimensional array is a list of one-dimensional arrays. The syntax for declaring a two dimensional array is as follows

```
Syntax:

<data-type> <array_name> [size1][size2];
```

where, *data-type* is the data type supported by C language, *array_name* is the identifier or array name, and *size1* and *size2* are sizes of the first and second index respectively. In other words, a two-dimensional array can be observed as a table which has *size1* number of rows and *size2* number of columns. Example: A two-dimensional array named *Mat* of 3 rows and 5 columns of data type *int* is declared as follows

```
int Mat[3][5];
```

The pictorial representation of the two-dimensional array *Mat* is shown in Fig 3.3.

	Col 0	Col 1	Col 2	Col 3	Col 4
Row 0	Mat[0][0]	Mat[0][1]	Mat[0][2]	Mat[0][3]	Mat[0][4]
Row 1	Mat[1][0]	Mat[1][1]	Mat[1][2]	Mat[1][3]	Mat[1][4]
Row 2	Mat[2][0]	Mat[2][1]	Mat[2][2]	Mat[2][3]	Mat[2][4]

Figure 3.3 Illustrating of elements and their address in two dimensional array

Like initialization of variables and one dimensional arrays, two dimensional arrays can be initialized after declaration as follows

```
int Matrix[2][3] = { {65, 80, 76}, {70, 50, 35}};
```

The commas separated values with nested braces { and } correspond to one of the row. However, the nested braces are optional. That is, following initialization is equal to above initialization.

```
int Matrix[2][3] = { 65, 80, 76, 70, 50, 35 };
```

Example: Write a C program to receive a values of matrix of dimension $M \times N$ and display the same.

```c
#include<stdio.h>

main()
{
int Matrix[100][100];
int i, j;


printf("Enter the dimension of the matrix\n");
printf("Rows :");
scanf("%d",&M);
printf("Columns :");
scanf("%d",&N);



/* Receive elements of first matrix from user */
printf("\nEnter the elements of matrix \n");
for(i = 0 ; i < M ; i++)
for(j = 0 ; j < N ; j++)
{
printf("Enter element of Matrix[%d][%d] = ", i,j);
scanf("%d",&Matrix[i][j]);
}



printf("\nUser provided matrix is \n");
for(i = 0 ; i < M ; i++)
{
for(j = 0 ; j < N ; j++)
printf("%5d", Matrix[i][j]);

printf("\n");
}


}


Output:

Enter the dimension of the matrix
Rows :3
Columns :4

Enter the elements of matrix
Enter element of Matrix[0][0] = 10
Enter element of Matrix[0][1] = 11
```

```
Enter element of Matrix[0][2] = 12
Enter element of Matrix[0][3] = 13
Enter element of Matrix[1][0] = 20
Enter element of Matrix[1][1] = 21
Enter element of Matrix[1][2] = 22
Enter element of Matrix[1][3] = 23
Enter element of Matrix[2][0] = 30
Enter element of Matrix[2][1] = 31
Enter element of Matrix[2][2] = 32
Enter element of Matrix[2][3] = 33

User provided matrix is
    10    11    12    13
    20    21    22    23
    30    31    32    33
```

Example: Write a program to receive two matrices from the user and provide the sum of corresponding elements.

```
#include<stdio.h>

main()
{
int MatOne[2][2], MatTwo[2][2];
int i, j, Result[2][2];

/* Receive elements of first matrix from user */
printf("Enter the elements of first matrix \n");
for(i = 0 ; i < 2 ; i++)
for(j = 0 ; j < 2 ; j++)
{
printf("Enter  MatOne[%d][%d] = ", i,j);
scanf("%d",&MatOne[i][j]);
}


/* Receive elements of second matrix from user */
printf("\nEnter the elements of second matrix \n");
for(i = 0 ; i < 2 ; i++)
for(j = 0 ; j < 2 ; j++)
{
printf("Enter  MatTwo[%d][%d] = ", i,j);
scanf("%d",&MatTwo[i][j]);
}


/* Compute sum of the both matrix */
for(i = 0 ; i < 2 ; i++)
for(j = 0 ; j < 2 ; j++)
Result[i][j] = MatOne[i][j] + MatTwo[i][j];
```

```
printf("\nMatrix sum is \n");
for(i = 0 ; i < 2 ; i++)
{
for(j = 0 ; j < 2 ; j++)
printf("%d\t", Result[i][j]);

printf("\n");
}


}
```

Output:

```
Enter the elements of first matrix
Enter  MatOne[0][0]:1
Enter  MatOne[0][1]:2
Enter  MatOne[1][0]:3
Enter  MatOne[1][1]:4

Enter the elements of second matrix
Enter  MatTwo[0][0]:5
Enter  MatTwo[0][1]:6
Enter  MatTwo[1][0]:7
Enter  MatTwo[1][1]:8

Matrix sum is
6   8
10   12
```

Chapter 4

STRINGS

Arrays can be classified based on its dimensions into one-dimensional or multi-dimensional. Similarly, based on the data type of the array, it can be classified into non-numerical and numerical. Where non-numerical is of *char* data type and it is numerical if the data type is of *int, float* or *double*. Non-numerical arrays which store *char* data type are also known as character array.

One-dimensional array of characters terminated by *null* character 0 is string. Some of the valid declaring and initialization of string is as follows

```
char name[] = "Badrinath";
char name[10] = "Badrinath";
char name[10] = {'B','a','d','r','i','n','a','t','h','\0'};
char name[] = {'B','a','d','r','i','n','a','t','h','\0'};
```

If the string is placed between double quotes *"Badrinath "*, explicitly providing of *null* character 0 is not required. The illustration of memory of above defined string are given in Fig 4.1.

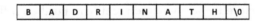

Figure 4.1 Illustrating of memory elements storing elements in string

An example C code to display initialized string and display string received from the user is as follows

```
#include<stdio.h>

main()
{
char Msg[] = "Hello", Txt[32];
Char Greet[10] = {'H','e','l','l','o','\0'};

printf("Hi user, your name:");
scanf("%s",Txt);

printf("\n%s %s\n", Msg, Txt);
printf("%s %s\n", Greet, Txt);
}
```

Output:

Run 1
Hi user, your name: Badri

Hello Badri
Hello Badri

4.1   READING AND PRINTING STRINGS

In C language, string data from the user is received using standard input devices such as keyboard and data is displayed to used on display unit.

4.1.1   String input

Following are the various function for reading string from user

- *scanf*()

- *getchar*()

- *gets*()

scanf   (): Generally, strings are read into the character array using *scanf* function using format specifier *%s* as follows

```
scanf("%s",Txt);
```

Note that *&* is not mentioned before the array name identifier. Further, if the user provides the input for *scanf* with multiple words (with string with white spaces), only first part of the string before white space is encountered is received and rest is ignored as shown in the example below

```
#include <stdio.h>

main()
{
char Txt[64];

printf("Enter string:");
scanf("%s",Txt);

printf("Input string is : %s", Txt);
}
```

Output:

Enter string: Badrinath Srinivas

```
Input string is : Badrinath
```

B	A	D	R	I	N	A	T	H		S	R	I	N	I	V	A	S	\0

Figure 4.2 Illustrating of storing string with white space

In the output, second part of the string *Srinivas* after white space is not displayed, because *scanf* function terminates as soon as white space is encountered. However, the string can contain white space while initialization as shown in Fig 4.2. Also, the entire string until the occurrence of *null* character will be printed using *printf* as illustrated in the following program.

```
#include <stdio.h>

main()
{
char Txt[] = "BADRINATH SRINIVAS";

printf("String is %s", Txt);
}

Output:

String is BADRINATH SRINIVAS
```

getchar : Generally, *getchar* is used to receive one character at a time. Example: Write a program to receive the text from user until enter key is pressed and then display the input string.

```
#include <stdio.h>

main()
{
char ch, Txt[64];
int i = 0;

printf("Enter line of text:");

do
{
ch = getchar();
Txt[i] = ch;
i = i + 1;
}while(ch != '\n')

Txt[i-1] = '\0';

printf("Input text is : %s", Txt);
}
```

Output:

```
Enter line of text: Badrinath Srinivas
Input text is : Badrinath Srinivas
```

Using the above program, complete line of text until enter key is invoked by user can be received. However, this process to take string is tedious.

gets : *gets* is used to read string. Example: Write a program to receive the text from user until enter key is pressed and then display the input string.

```
#include <stdio.h>
#include <string.h>
main()
{
char Txt[64];

printf("Enter line of text:");
gets(Txt);
printf("Input text is : %s", Txt);
}
```

Output:

```
Enter line of text: Badrinath Srinivas
Input text is : Badrinath Srinivas
```

4.1.2 String output

Following are the various function for printing string

- *printf()*

- *putchar()*

- *puts()*

printf : This function is most widely used function in C programming. It prints the string and numerical values as per the format specified. Example:

```
#include <stdio.h>
main()
{
char Txt[64] = "Badrinath Srinivas";

printf("First time string is : %s ", Txt);
printf("Second time string is : %s ", Txt);
}
```

Output:

```
First time string is : Badrinath Srinivas Second time string is : Badrinath Srinivas
```

putchar   : This function is subset of *printf*. It is used to display one character of the string.

```
#include <stdio.h>
#include <conio.h>
main()
{
char Txt[64] = "Badrinath Srinivas";

putchar(Txt[0]);
putchar(Txt[8]);
putchar(Txt[10]);
}
```

Output:

BhS

puts   : This function displays string to stdout appending newline to the output.

```
#include <stdio.h>
#include <conio.h>
main()
{
char Txt[64] = "Badrinath Srinivas";

puts(Txt);
puts(Txt);
}
```

Output:

```
Badrinath Srinivas
Badrinath Srinivas
```


4.2   STRING HANDLING FUNCTIONS

In this section, *null* terminated string manipulation functions provided in C language are discussed. These string handling functions are implemented in header file *string.h*. To invoke these functions, *string.h* header file has to be included as follows


```
#include <string.h>
```


strlen   (): This function returns the length of the string. The string length does not include the *null* character ′0′. The syntax for *strlen* function is as follows

```
Length = strlen(Text);
```

where, *strlen* is the function name and *Text* is string. **Example:** Determine the length of string

```
#include<stdio.h>
#include <string.h>
main()
{
char Text[32] = "Badrinath";
int Length;

Length = strlen(Text);
printf("Length = :%d",Length);
}
```

```
Output:
Length = 9
```

strcpy   (): This function copies the string from one variable to other variable. The syntax for *strcpy* function is as follows

```
Length = strcpy(Destination, Source);
```

where, *strcpy* is the function name and contents from character array variable *Source* or string constant is copied to character array variable *Destination*. **Example:** Copy the string from one variable to other variable

```
#include<stdio.h>
#include <string.h>
main()
{
char Source[32] = "Bangalore", Dest[32] = "Delhi";

printf(" Source = %s, Dest = %s \n", Source, Dest);
strcpy(Dest, Source);
printf(" Source = %s, Dest = %s", Source, Dest);
}
```

```
Output:
Source = Bangalore, Dest = Delhi
Source = Bangalore, Dest = Bangalore
```

strcat   (): This function appends the string from one variable or string constant to other string variable. The syntax for *strcat* function is as follows

```
strcat(Destination, Source);
```

where, *strcat* is the function name and contents from string variable *Source* is appended to string variable *Destination*. **Example:** Concatenate the string from one variable to other variable

```
#include<stdio.h>
#include <string.h>
main()
{
char Dest[32] = "Srinivas", Source[32] = "Badrinath";

printf(" Source = %s, Dest = %s \n", Source, Dest);
strcat(Dest, Source);
printf(" Source = %s, Dest = %s", Source, Dest);
}
```

```
Output:
Source = Badrinath, Dest = Srinivas
Source = Badrinath Srinivas, Dest = Srinivas
```

strcmp (): This function compares the two string character by character sequentially and return zero if both are same. Otherwise, it returns non zero value. The syntax for *strcmp* function is as follows

```
Result = strcmp(First_String, Second_String);
```

where, *strcmp* is the function name, *First_String* and *Second_String* are strings to be compared against each other, and Result is a integer value returned after comparison. **Example:** Compare two string

```
#include<stdio.h>
#include <string.h>
main()
{
char First[32], Second[32];
int Result;

printf("First string:");
scanf("%s",First);

printf("Second string:");
scanf("%s",Second);

Result = strcmp(First, Second);

if(Result == 0)
printf(" First = %s and Second = %s are Same\n", First, Second);
else
```

```
printf(" First = %s and Second = %s are Different\n", First, Second);
}
```

Output:

Run1
First string: Badrinath
Second string: Srinivas

First = Badrinath and Second = Srinivas are Different

Run2
First string: Badrinath
Second string: Badrinath

First = Badrinath and Second = Badrinath are Same

strcmpi (): This function is similar to function *strcmp* compares the two strings character by character the case. The syntax for *strcmp* function is as follows

```
Result = strcmpi(First_String, Second_String);
```

where, *strcmpi* is the function name, *First_String* and *Second_String* are strings to be compared against each other, and *Result* is a integer value returned after comparison. **Example:** Compare two strings ignoring the case

```
#include<stdio.h>
#include <string.h>
main()
{
char First[32], Second[32];
int Result;

printf("First string:");
scanf("%s",First);

printf("Second string:");
scanf("%s",Second);

Result = strcmpi(First, Second);

if(Result == 0)
printf(" First = %s and Second = %s are Same\n", First, Second);
else
printf(" First = %s and Second = %s are Different\n", First, Second);
}
```

Output:

Run1
First string: Badrinath
Second string: BADRINATH

First = Badrinath and Second = BADRINATH are Same

strlwr (): This function converts all the upper case characters of the *string* to lower case. The syntax for *strlwr* function is as follows

```
Converted = strlwr(Source);
```

where, *strlwr* is the function name, *Source* and *Converted* are the strings before and after converting the upper case characters in to lower case respectively. **Example:** Convert the upper case characters to lower case

```
#include<stdio.h>
#include <string.h>
main()
{
char First[32], Result[32];

printf("Input string:");
scanf("%s",First);

Result = strlwr(First);

printf(" Before = %s and After conversion = %s\n", First, Result);
}
```

Output:

Run1
Input string : Badrinath
Before = Badrinath and After conversion = badrinath

strupr (): This function converts all the lower case characters of the input *string* to upper case. The syntax for *strupr* function is as follows

```
Converted = strupr(Source);
```

where, *strupr* is the function name, *Source* and *Converted* are the strings before and after converting the lower case characters into upper case respectively. **Example:** Convert the upper case characters to lower case

```
#include<stdio.h>
```

```
#include <string.h>
main()
{
char First[32], Result[32];

printf("Input string:");
scanf("%s",First);

Result = strupr(First);

printf(" Before = %s and After conversion = %s\n", First, Result);
}
```

Output:

```
Run1
Input string : Badrinath
Before = Badrinath and After conversion = BADRINATH
```

strrev (): This function reverses all characters of the input string. The syntax for *strrev* function is as follows

```
Reversed = strrev(Input);
```

where, *strrev* is the function name, *Input* and *Reversed* are the input string and reversed input string respectively. **Example:** Reverse the input string

```
#include<stdio.h>
#include <string.h>
main()
{ char First[32], Result[32];

printf("Input string:");
scanf("%s",First);

Result = strrev(First);

printf(" Original = %s and Reversed = %s\n", First, Result);
}
```

Output:

```
Run1
Input string : Badrinath
Original = Badrinath and Reversed = htanirdaB
```

4.3 ARRAY OF STRINGS

Array of strings is array of character strings. Declaration and initialization of arrays of strings is as follows.

```
char array_name [array_size][string_size]
```

where, *array_name* is the identifier variable, *array_size* is the size of the array and *string_size* is length of the each string in the array. Declaration and initialization of array of strings is as follows

```
char Names[5][16] = {"Badrinath", "Srinivas", "Chandrakant", "Bangalore", "New Delhi"};
```

B	a	d	r	i	n	a	t	H	\0						
S	r	i	n	i	v	a	s	\0							
C	h	a	n	d	r	a	k	a	n	t	\0				
B	a	n	g	a	l	o	r	e	\0						
N	e	w		D	e	l	h	i	\0						

Figure 4.3 Illustrating of memory of arrays of strings

Here *Names* is arrays of strings with each name of maximum length not exceeding 15 characters. It can be visualized using two dimensional character arrays as shown in Fig 4.3. It has five names. But accessing individual name is using single subscript. For example, *Names* [0] gives the entire character array *Badri*.

Example: Write a C program to receive names of the operating systems and display the same in reverse order.

```
#include<stdio.h>
main()
{
char OS_Names[32][32];
int N;

printf("Enter the number of Operating systems:");
scanf("%d",&N);

for(i = 0; i < N ; i++)
scanf("%s",OS_Names[i]);

printf("Names of the Operating systems are\n");
for(i = 0; i < N ; i++)
printf("%d.\t%s",i, OS_Names[i]);

}

Output:
Run1

Enter the number of Operating systems: 5
Windows
Linux
Android
```

QNX
iOS

Names of the Operating systems are
1. Windows
2. Linux
3. Android
4. QNX
5. iOS

Chapter 5

FUNCTIONS

Complex task can be automatized using a large program. Large task can be segmented to sub-tasks. Further, in large task, same sub-tasks need to computed multiple times at different instances at various conditions. Then same code appears multiple times. Thus, coding complex large task using large single program has problems such as (i) Code re-usability is low or Redundancy of code because sub-tasks are coded multiple times, (ii) Debugging and testing becomes complex because bug found has to corrected or updated at all places of the same sub-task in the large code and (iii) Lack of readability.

The large task or program can be systematically divided into small sub-tasks or programs. Where each sub-task is called as module. This approach of systematically dividing the large task or program into small programs or sub-tasks is known as modularisation or structured programming. C language supports *functions* which are used to achieve modular or structured programming.

Functions are blocks of code to perform a well defined task. For example, a task can be to compute the factorial of a given number or product of two numbers. C programming has two types of functions known as (i) Library functions and (ii) User defined functions. Following are some of the characteristics of the function

- Each function is independent to other functions

- A function can call any other function or itself

- After completion of execution of the function, the control returns back to instruction or statement which invoked to current function

- Function can receive any number of input values as arguments from invoking instruction or statement.

- Function can return single value or nothing to invoking instruction or statement.

5.0.1 Library functions

Library functions are *built-in* functions which are provided along with C compiler. These functions are already implemented and user need not worry about them. These functions perform predefined tasks and all built-in functions return a value. To use these functions you have to include appropriate header files. Following are some of the built-in or library functions

- *scanf()* : *stdio.h* : Read the data from the standard output

- *printf()* : *stdio.h* : Display the data on the standard output

- *sqrt()* : *math.h* : Computes the square root of a number

71

- *clrscr*() : *conio.h* : Clear the output screen

- *strlen*() : *string.h* : Determine the length of the string

- *pow*() : *math.h* : Computes the exponential value of a number

For example, write a program to compute the exponential of a number and display the same using built-in or library functions.

```
#include <stdio.h>/* for scanf and printf functions */
#include <math.h>  /* for pow() function */

main()
{
int Res, Base, Exp;

printf("Enter the number:");
scanf(:%d",&Base);

printf("Enter the exponent:");
scanf(:%d",&Exp);

Res = pow(Base, Exp);

printf("Result is %d", Res);

}

Output:
Enter the number: 2
Enter the exponent: 5
Result is 32
```

5.1   USER DEFINED FUNCTIONS

C language allows programmer to create a function according to the requirements. These functions are known as user-defined functions. For example, programmer can write his/her own functions to (i) find factorial of a number and to (ii) determine whether the given number is odd or even. The function *func1* which invokes another function *func2* are known as *calling* function and *called* function respectively. Each user defined function and its use in the program has following aspects

- Function definition

- Function declaration

- Function call

5.1.1   Function definition

Function definition is the actual sub-task performing specific task using set of instructions. The general form of a function definition in C programming language is as follows:

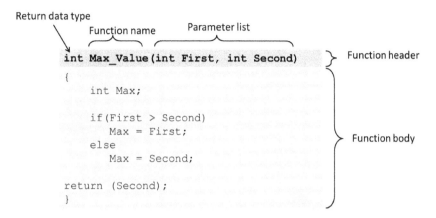

Figure 5.1 Illustration of *function body* and *function header*

```
return_data_type function_name( parameter list)
{
    Declaration of local variables

    Code block /* Executable statements */

    return (Expression or Variable)
}
```

where, the code between the braces { and } is known as *function body*, and the first line of function including *function_name*, *return_data_type* and *parameter list* is known *function header*. Graphical illustration of *function body* and *function header* is shown in Fig 5.1. Each section of function are described below

- *function_name*: It is the name of the function or identifier of the function. *function_name* is used by *calling* function to invoke the function.

- *return*: It is a keyword used to send the result or value to the *calling function*.

- *Declaration of local variables*: These are variables declared in the function for performing the task.

- *Code block*: Executable instructions which perform the actual task.

- *return_data_type*: Indicate the data type of the *return* value from the function. Data type can be of *int*, *float*, *char*, etc. Sometimes function does not return any value. Then, *return_data_type* is *void*.

- *parameter list* : These are set of variables which receive values that are passed from *calling* function to this function. These parameters specify the type and order similar to the corresponding arguments mentioned in the calling function. These parameter values might be used in the *code block* for completion of the task. However, parameters list are optional. That is, function need not have parameters.

Example: Write a function which receives two variables and determines the max of the them.

```
int Max_Value(int First, int Second)
{
```

```
int Max;

if(First > Second)
Max = First;
else
Max = Second;

return (Max);
}
```

5.1.2   Function declaration

Similar to declaring variables before being used, functions should be declared before they are used in the functions it is called. It informs the compilers that such function exists and may be used during the execution of the program. The syntax for function declaration is as follows

```
return_data_type function_name( parameter list);
```

It is similar to function header with semicolon as the terminating statement. However, the *parameter list* has the data type of variables in order, and does not have the variable names. Function declaration for the above example is as follows

```
main()
{
int Max_Value(int, int); /* Declaration */

. . .
. . .

}

/* Function definition */

int Max_Value(int First, int Second)
{
int Max; /* Local Variable */

if(First > Second)
Max = First;
else
Max = Second;

return (Second); /* Return value */
}
```

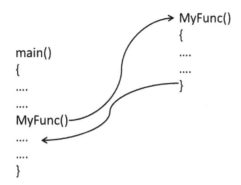

Figure 5.2 Illustrating of flow of control

5.1.3   Function call

To use a function which is defined and declared, it has to invoked with appropriate arguments. Invoking a function is known as function call. When a function is invoked the control is passed to function definition and control returns when *return* is invoked in the *called function*. Graphical illustration of flow of control is shown in Fig 5.2. The function can be invoked with (i) arguments or (ii) without arguments. Function declaration for the above example is as follows

```
#include<stdio.h>

main()
{
int F,S, Result;
int Max_Value(int, int); /* Declaration */

printf("Enter first number");
scanf("%d",&F);

printf("Enter second number");
scanf("%d",&S);

Result = Max_Value(F,S);   /* Function call */

printf("Maximum of two numbers if %d",Result);

}

/* Function definition */

int Max_Value(int First, int Second)
{
int Max; /* Local Variable */

if(First > Second)
Max = First;
else
```

```
Max = Second;

return (Second); /* Return value */
}
```

Example: Write a program to find the factorial of the numbers from *x* to *y*.

```
#include<stdio.h>

main()
{
int Fst,Snd, Result;
int j;
int MyFact(int);      /* Declaration */

printf("Enter first number:");
scanf("%d",&Fst);

printf("Enter second number:");
scanf("%d",&Snd);

for (j = Fst; j <= Snd ; j++)
{
Result = MyFact(j);  /* Function call */
printf("Factorial of %d is %d \n",j, Result);
}

}

/* Function definition */

int MyFact(int Num)
{
int Result = 1;
int i; /* Local Variables */

for(i = Num ; i > 1 ; i-- )
Result = (Result * i);


return (Result); /* Return value */
}

Output:

Enter first number:3
Enter second number:7

Factorial of 3 is 6
Factorial of 4 is 24
```

```
Factorial of 5 is 120
Factorial of 6 is 720
Factorial of 7 is 5040
```

5.2   ARGUMENTS AND PARAMETERS

Arguments and parameters are the means for communicating data or address from calling function to called function. Variables listed in the *function call* are known as arguments and variables listed in the *function header* are known as *parameters*. *Parameters* receive values from *arguments* from *function call*. Parameters are also called *formal parameters* or *actual parameters*. Following C program to compute the cube of the number *N*, illustrates the arguments, parameters and return value .

```
#include<stdio.h>

main()
{
int N, Result;
int MyCube(int);      /* Declaration */

printf("Enter number:");
scanf("%d",&N);

Result = MyCube(N);   /* Function call. N is the Argument */
printf("Cube of %d is %d \n",N, Result);


}

/* Function definition */

int MyCube(int Num) /* Num is the parameter */
{
int Result; /* Local Variables */

Result = Num * Num * Num;


return (Result); /* Return value. Result is returned to calling function */
}

Output:

Run1
Enter number:3
Cube of 3 is 27

Run2
Enter number:5
Cube of 5 is 125
```

5.3   CATEGORIES OF FUNCTION

Based on *parameters* and *return* value, functions are classified into four categories as follows

- Function with no arguments and no return value

- Function with no arguments and return value

- Function with arguments but no return value

- Function with arguments and return value

5.3.1   Function with no arguments and no return value

This is the simplest form of function, which neither takes any arguments from *calling function* nor *return* any value to *calling function*. Thus, there are no arguments in function call and parameters in the function header. Following is an example program with a function to determine weather the user provided number is odd or even and return nothing.

```c
#include<stdio.h>

main()
{
void OddEven();      /* Declaration */

OddEven(); /* Function call with no arguments */

}

/* Function definition */

void OddEven() /* Function header with no parameters */
{
int Num; /* Local Variables */

printf("Enter a number:",&Num);

if( Num%2 == 0)
printf(" %d is Even",Num);
else
printf(" %d is Odd",Num);

/* Returns nothing */
}
```

Output:

Run1
Enter a number:66

```
66 is Even
```

```
Run2
Enter number:55
55 is Odd
```

5.3.2 Function with arguments and no return value

This form of function takes arguments from *calling function* and does not *return* any value to *calling function*. Thus, there are arguments in function call and parameters in the function header. However, there is no *return* statement in the *called function*. Following is an example program with a function which takes parameter and determines weather the user provided number is odd or even and return nothing.

```c
#include<stdio.h>

main()
{
int Num;
void OddEven();      /* Declaration */

printf("Enter a number:");
scanf("%d",&Num);

OddEven(Num); /* Function call with arguments */

}

/* Function definition */

void OddEven(int LocalPar) /* Function header with one parameter */
{

if( LocalPar%2 == 0)
printf(" %d is Even",LocalPar);
else
printf(" %d is Odd",LocalPar);

/* Returns nothing */
}
```

```
Output:

Run1
Enter a number:66
66 is Even

Run2
Enter number:55
55 is Odd
```

5.3.3   Function with no arguments and return value

In this category, function does not take arguments from *calling function*, but *returns* a value to *calling function*. Thus, there are no arguments in function call and parameters in the function header. However, there is *return* statement in the *called function*. Following is an example program with a function which takes no parameters and return maximum of two numbers received by user to calling function.

```c
#include<stdio.h>

main()
{
int Result;
int MyMax();      /* Declaration */

Result = MyMax(); /* Function call with no arguments */
printf("Maximum number is %d",Result);

}

/* Function definition */

int MyMax() /* Function header with no parameters */
{
int Fst, Snd, Res;

printf("First Number :");
scanf("%d",&Fst);

printf("Second Number :");
scanf("%d",&Snd);

if( Fst > Snd )
Res = Fst;
else
Res = Snd;

return(Res); /* Returns maximum of two numbers */
}

Output:

First Number: 10
Second Number: 30
Maximum number is 30
```

5.3.4   Function with arguments and return value

In this category, function takes arguments from *calling function* and also *returns* a value to *calling function*. Thus, there are arguments in function call and parameters in the function header. Also, there is *return* statement in the *called function*. Following is an example program with a function which takes two variables as parameters and return maximum value of these two variables to calling function.

```
#include<stdio.h>

main()
{
int First, Second, Result;
int MyMax(int, int);      /* Declaration */

printf("First Number :");
scanf("%d",&First);

printf("First Number :");
scanf("%d",&Second);


Result = MyMax(First, Second); /* Function call with arguments */
printf("Maximum number is %d",Result);

}

/* Function definition */

int MyMax(int Fst, int Snd) /* Function header with two parameters */
{
int Res;

if( Fst > Snd )
Res = Fst;
else
Res = Snd;

return(Res); /* Returns maximum of two numbers */
}

Output:
Run1

First Number: 54
Second Number: 23
Maximum number is 54
```

5.4   ARGUMENT PASSING TO FUNCTIONS

When a function is invoked with arguments the called function with parameters of corresponding data type much be declared. These parameters in called function are known as actual parameters or formal parameters. Formal parameters are created as soon as control enters the called function. These formal parameters are local variables inside the called function. However, these formal parameters are destroyed upon exit of called function. Further, when function is called the arguments are passed to a function to a function in two methods as follows

- Call by value

- Call by reference

5.4.1   Call by value

In this type of passing arguments, the actual value of the arguments are copied into the formal parameters of the calling function. The changes made to the parameters inside the called function have no effect on the actual arguments in the calling function. By default, C programming uses call by value method to pass arguments. An example program to illustrate call by value which does not have effect on the actual arguments is discussed using function *swap()* as follows.

```c
#include <stdio.h>

main()
{

int Fst, Snd;
void MySwap(int, int);

printf("Enter first number:");
scanf("%d",&Fst);

printf("Enter second number:");
scanf("%d",&Snd);

printf("Before swap: First number is %d and Second number is %d\n",Fst, Snd);
MySwap(Fst, Snd);
printf("After swap: First number is %d and Second number is %d",Fst, Snd);

}

void MySwap(int First, int Second)
{
int Temp;

Temp = First;
First = Second;
Second = Temp;

}
```

```
Output:
Run1

Enter first number: 100
Enter second number: 543
Before swap: First number is 100 and Second number is 543
After swap: First number is 100 and Second number is 543


Run2

Enter first number: 234
Enter second number: 789
Before swap: First number is 234 and Second number is 789
After swap: First number is 789 and Second number is 234
```

5.4.2   Call by reference

In this type of passing arguments, the *actual address* of the arguments are copied into the formal parameters of the calling function. Thus the changes made to the actual parameters inside the called function will reflect in the actual arguments of the calling function. An example program to illustrate call by reference which reflect the changes in the calling function is discussed using function *swap()* as follows.

```
#include <stdio.h>

main()
{

int Fst, Snd;
void MySwap(int*, int*);

printf("Enter first number:");
scanf("%d",&Fst);

printf("Enter second number:");
scanf("%d",&Snd);

printf("Before swap: First number is %d and Second number is %d\n",Fst, Snd);
MySwap(&Fst, &Snd);
printf("After swap: First number is %d and Second number is %d",Fst, Snd);

}

void MySwap(int *First, int *Second)
{
int Temp;
```

```
Temp = *First;
*First = *Second;
*Second = Temp;


}

Output:
Run1

Enter first number: 100
Enter second number: 543
Before swap: First number is 100 and Second number is 543
After swap: First number is 543 and Second number is 100

Run2

Enter first number: 234
Enter second number: 789
Before swap: First number is 234 and Second number is 789
After swap: First number is 789 and Second number is 234
```

5.4.3 Using arrays with functions

Passing arrays to function: Generally, when variables are passed as arguments, the values are copied into parameters of called function. However, when array variables are passed as arguments, the base address of array is copied into the parameters of called function. In C language, by default, arrays are always passed by reference. Since arrays are passed by reference, any changes made to array received parameters in the called function reflects in the calling function. The formal parameters can be declared in the called function in three different methods as follows

- Pointer

- Sized array

- Unsized array

Receiving the array as parameters using all the above mentioned three approaches are illustrated using the following example. Consider the following function *MyMean*, where array of size *10* is passed as argument to the function as follows.

```
main()
{
int Number[10];
void MyMean(int *);
...
...
MyMean(Number);


}
```

Pointer: Receiving the array as formal parameter using pointer as follows

```
void MyMean(int *MyArr)
{
...
...
}
```

Sized array: Receiving the array as formal parameter as sized array as follows

```
void MyMean(int MyArr[10])
{
...
...
}
```

Unsized array: Receiving the array as formal parameter as unsized array as follows

```
void MyMean(int MyArr[])
{
...
...
}
```

Example: Write a C program where a function takes array of numbers as argument and compute the square of each numbers Also, illustrate that the modification of array are reflected in the main function.

```
#include <stdio.h>

main()
{

int Number[5], i, Fst, Snd, Temp;
void MySwap_Square(int, int, int*);

printf("Enter first number:");
scanf("%d",&Fst);

printf("Enter second number:");
scanf("%d",&Snd);

printf("Enter the values whose square is required:");
for( i = 0; i < 5 ; i++)
{
printf("%d number:",i+1);
scanf("%d",&Number[i]);
```

```
}

printf("\nBefore passing for the function \n");
printf("First Number is %d and Second number %d\n", Fst, Snd);
printf("The values whose squares required are \n");
for( i = 0; i < 5 ; i++)
    printf("%d \t",Number[i]);


MySwap_Square(Fst,Snd,Number);

printf("\nAfter passing for the function \n");
printf("First Number is %d and Second number %d\n", Fst, Snd);
printf("The square of the values are \n");
for( i = 0; i < 5 ; i++)
printf("%d \t",Number[i]);


}

void MySwap_Square(int First, int Second, int *NumSquare)
{
int Temp, i;

Temp = First;
First = Second;
Second = Temp;

for( i = 0; i < 5 ; i++)
NumSquare[i] = NumSquare[i] * NumSquare[i];

}


Output:
Run1

Enter first number: 100
Enter second number: 543
Before swap: First number is 100 and Second number is 543
After swap: First number is 543 and Second number is 100

Run2

Enter first number: 234
Enter second number: 789
Before swap: First number is 234 and Second number is 789
After swap: First number is 789 and Second number is 234
```

Return array from function: C programming language does not allow to *return* more than one value. So, array can be returned to main program by specifying the arrays address. In other words, return arrays name without index as follows. An example to illustrate returning array from function is as follows.

```
main()
{

int *RetArray; /* pointer variable to receive the address of the array from function */
int* MyArray(void); /* function declaration */

...
...

RetArray = MyArray(); /* Receive the address of the array from the function */
}


int* MyArray(void) /* return type is address of array */
{
static int MyArray[10]; /* Local array that will be returned */
...
...
return (MyArray) /* return array name */
}
```

Example: Write a C program to receive the values from user in a function and return the array storing the values to the main function.

```
#include <stdio.h>
main()
{
int i;
int *RetArray; /* pointer variable to receive the address of the array from function */
int* MyArray(void); /* function declaration */

RetArray = MyArray(); /* Receive the address of the array from the function */

printf("Main function \n The values provided are \n");
for (i = 0; i< 10 ; i++)
printf("%d, \t",i+1, RetArray[i]);


}


int* MyArray(void) /* return type is address of array */
{
int j;
static int MyArray[10]; /* Local array that will be returned */
printf(" Control in user defined function \n Enter 10 values \n");
```

```
for (j = 0; j < 10 ; j++)
scanf("%d",&MyArray[j]);

return (MyArray); /* return array name */
}
```

Output

```
User defined function
Enter 10 values
10 20 30 40 50 60 70 80 90 100

Main function
The values provided are
10,20,30,40,50,60,70,80,90,100,
```

5.5 RECURSIONS

Recursion is a programming technique which allows the programmer to express operations in terms of function itself. It is similar to a loop, which repeats the same function code invoked from itself. However, there must be a terminating or stopping condition in the recursive function. Otherwise the recursive call does not terminate and enters into infinite loop. Following gives the illustration for invoking a function as recursion

```
void main()
{
    MyFunc();
}

void MyFunc()
{
if( terminating condition )
    return ;
    else
    MyFunc(); /* function calls itself */
}
```

Recursive function are useful to solve mathematical problems such as to calculate factorial of a number, generating Fibonacci series, etc. Example: Write a C program to compute the factorial of a number using recursive calls

```
#include <stdio.h>
int main()
{
int Num, Result;
int MyFact(int);
```

```
printf("Enter a positive number :");
scanf("%d",&Num);

Result = MyFact(Num);
printf("Factorial of %d is %d", Num, Result);

}

int MyFact(int N)
{
if( N <= 1)
    return 1;
    else
    return ( MyFact( N - 1 ) * N );  /* function calls itself */
}

Output:
Run1
Enter a positive number : 4
Factorial of 4 is 24

Run2
Enter a positive number : 7
Factorial of 7 is 5040
```

Example: Write a C program to compute the sum of first N natural numbers using recursive calls.

```
#include <stdio.h>
int main()
{
int Num, Result;
int MySum(int);

printf("Enter a positive number :");
scanf("%d",&Num);

Result = MySum(Num);
printf("Sum of numbers upto %d is %d", Num, Result);

}

int MySum(int N)
{
if( N == 1)
    return 1;
    else
    return ( MySum( N - 1 ) + N );  /* function calls itself */
}
```

```
Output:
Run1
Enter a positive number : 5
Factorial of 5 is 15

Run2
Enter a positive number : 10
Factorial of 10 is 55
```

5.6   LOCATION OF FUNCTIONS

The location of the function definition defined in the C program is important for its inclusion in the *main* program. Further, the function declaration for inclusion in the *main* function is also dependent on the location of the function definition. However, the programmer can define function at following three different locations

- Functions after the *main*() function

- Functions before the *main*() function

- Function definition in the different files

5.6.1   Functions after the main function

In this method, the function definition is written after the main function. Since, the function is written after main function, the main is not aware of the function. Thus, we need to declare the function inside the main function or before main function. All the programs mentioned in this chapter are of this approach. Example program to illustrate function after main function is given below.

```
#include <stdio.h>
int main()
{
int Num, Result;
int MySquare(int);

printf("Enter a positive number :");
scanf("%d",&Num);

Result = MySquare(Num);
printf("Square of %d is %d", Num, Result);

}

int MySquare(int N)
{
return(N * N);
}

Output:
Run1
```

```
Enter a positive number : 5
Square of 5 is 25

Run2
Enter a positive number : 10
Square of 10 is 100
```

5.6.2 Functions before the main function

In this method, the function definition is written before the main function. However, function should be defined after pre-processor statements such as **#include<stdio.h>**. Since, the function is written before main function, the main is aware of the function. Thus, there is no need to declare the function before invoking. Example program to illustrate function definition before main function is given below.

```c
#include <stdio.h>

int MySquare(int N)
{
return(N * N);
}

/* Function declaration is not required */
int main()
{
int Num, Result;

printf("Enter a positive number :");
scanf("%d",&Num);

Result = MySquare(Num);
printf("Square of %d is %d", Num, Result);

}
```

```
Output:
Run1
Enter a positive number : 5
Square of 5 is 25

Run2
Enter a positive number : 10
Square of 10 is 100
```

5.6.3   Function definition in the different files

Generally, small programs can be coded in same file. However, large tasks will be shared with many people. Thus, each programmer would code the functions which performs sub-tasks in different files. Finally, all the files are compiled together for execution of large task. These files (**myfile**) should have extension with **.c**. These files should be included as a pre-processor statement like **#include "myfile.c"**. For example, let the function for computing square *MySquare* is defined in file *MyCode.c*. Illustration for including the function in main is as follows

```c
#include <stdio.h>
#include "MyCode.c" /* File with function MySquare is included */

/* Function declaration is not required */
int main()
{
int Num, Result;

printf("Enter a positive number :");
scanf("%d",&Num);

Result = MySquare(Num);
printf("Square of %d is %d", Num, Result);

}

Output:
Run1
Enter a positive number : 5
Square of 5 is 25

Run2
Enter a positive number : 10
Square of 10 is 100
```

Chapter 6

Storage classes and Scope of variables

A storage class tells us where the variable would be stored, what would be the initial value of the variable if no value is assigned, what is the life time of the variable and scope of the variable. Scope of the variable refers to where variables can be referenced or where it can be accessed by name.

Basically there are four storage classes in C as shown in figure 7.1 : Automatic, Register, Static and External storage classes.

6.1 AUTOMATIC VARIABLES

Automatic Variables also called as Local Variables, the keyword used for Automatic storage class is "auto". The default value of Automatic variable is garbage value and the scope of that variable is local to the block wherein the variable is defined. Automatic Variable is available till the control remains inside the block wherein the variable id defined.

Memory for Automatic Variable is allocated automatically upon admission to a block and de-allocated/freed automatically upon exit from the block.

Example:

```
#include<stdio.h>
    int main(){
    auto int a;
    printf("%d\n",a);
    a=123;
    printf("%d",a);
    return 0;
    }
```
Output:
0
123

In the above program, the first *printf* will output a garbage value and second *printf* will display assigned value i.e, 123.

6.2 REGISTER VARIABLES

Register variable is similar to Automatic variable where register keyword is used to define local variables that must be stored in a CPU register rather than RAM. Primary difference between auto and register is that variable declared as auto is stored in memory whereas variable declared as register is stored in CPU

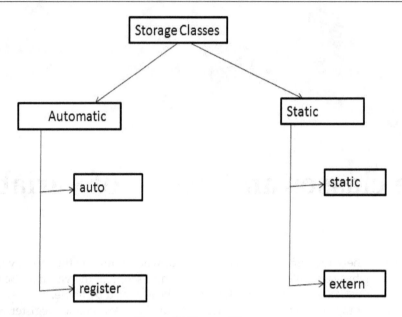

Figure 6.1 Storage Classes

register. Here too default value of register variable is garbage value. Generally register should only be used for variables that need fast access - like counters since accessing data in memory is significantly slower than processing in the CPU.

Register variables are allocated storage upon admission to a block; and the storage is de-allocated when the block is exited. The scope of register variables is local to the block wherein they are declared.

The number of CPU registers is restricted; if the allocated CPU register is busy doing some other task then variable might operate as automatic variable.

Example:

```
#include<stdio.h>
    int main(){
    register int a;
    printf("%d\n",a);
    a=123;
    printf("%d",a);
    return 0;
}
Output:
0
123
```

In the above program, the first *printf* will output a garbage value and second *printf* will display assigned value i.e, 123.

6.3   EXTERNAL VARIABLES

The External Variable is used to provide a reference to a global variable that is visible to all the programs. The keyword used for External storage class is "extern". The scope of external variables is global, i.e. the whole code in the file following the declarations. Any functions in the program may access the external variable by using its name. External Variable is living as long as the execution of program does not come to an end. Default value of External Variable is zero.

Example:

```
#include<stdio.h>
int i;
int main(){
    extern int e;
    printf("%d \n %d",i,e);
return 0;
}
int e=100;Output:
Output:
0
100
```

6.4 STATIC VARIABLES

The static variable is a default storage class for global variables. The static variable is visible within all functions in this source file. The keyword used for Static storage class is static. Static storage class is declared with the keyword static. These variables are automatically initialized to 0 upon memory allocation. Life of variable perseveres between different function calls. The static storage class provides a lifetime over the whole program.

Example:

```
#include<stdio.h>
void method(void);
static count=5;
int main()
{
while (count--)
{
method();
}
return 0;
}
void method( void )
{
static i = 2;
i++;
printf("i is %d and count is %d\n", i, count);
}
Output:
i is 3 and count is 4
i is 4 and count is 3
i is 5 and count is 2
i is 6 and count is 1
i is 7 and count is 0
```

All above storage classes are highlighted in the table 6.1.

Feature/ Storage Type	auto	register	extern	static
Definition	Local variable known to only to the function.	Local variable which is stored in the register.	Global variable known to all functions in the file.	Local variable which retains its value even after the control is transferred to the calling function.
Declaration syntax	auto data_type variable_name;	register data_type variable_name;	extern data_type variable_name;	static data_type variable_name;
Accessibility	Within the function or block.	within the function or block where it is declared.	Within the combination of program modules.	Within the program/function/block where it is declared.
Storage	Primary memory	Register of CPU	Primary memory	Primary memory
Default Value	Garbage	Garbage	Zero	Zero

Table 6.1 Storage Classes of Variables

Chapter 7

Structures

Structure in C is a collection of different data types (user defined or primitive data types) which are grouped together and each element in a C structure is called member. Structure variable should be declared to access structure members in C, memory will be allocated for each member separately. Syntax of structure followed by an example is shown below,

```
[typedef] struct [struct_name]
{
    type attribute1;
    type attribute2;
    // other members
    [struct struct_name *struct_instance;]
} [struct_name_t] [struct_instance];
```

Example:

```
struct Books
{
    int     id;
    char    title[40];
    char    author[40];
    float   price;
} book;
```

A pictorial representation of structure is shown in figure 7.1. We need to remember following points while using C structures,

(a) *struct* is a keyword, we must use this keyword to declare a structure.

(b) Members of structure should be enclosed within opening and closing braces.

(c) Declaration of Structure reserves no space.

(d) Structure will act as a "Template/Map/Shape", so whole container is available for every structure instance.

(e) Memory is created very first time when the instance is created.

C structure is more powerful compare to C variable and C array, C structure can hold multi-variables of different data types(int, char, float, double and long double), where as a normal variable can hold only one data of one data type at a time and an array can hold group of data of same data type.
Example:

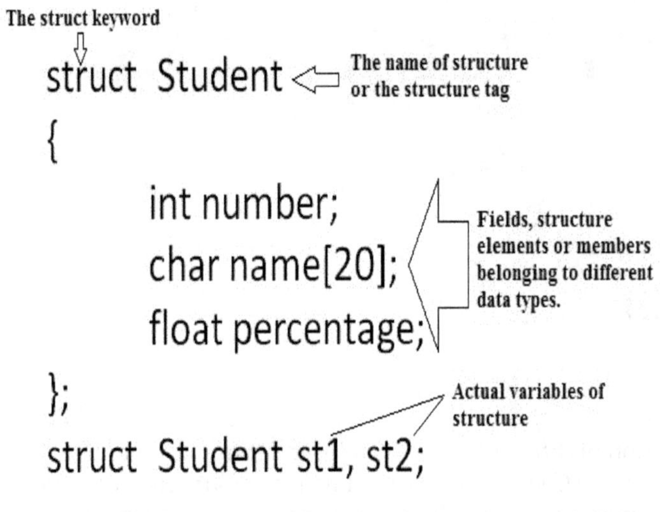

The struct keyword

struct Student ⇐ The name of structure or the structure tag

{

    int number;

    char name[20]; ⟨ Fields, structure elements or members belonging to different data types.

    float percentage;

};

struct Student st1, st2; — Actual variables of structure

Figure 7.1 Structure

```c
#include <stdio.h>
struct Student
{
        int rollNo;
        char name[40];
        float percentage;
};

int main()
{
        struct Student stu = {0}; //Initializing to null

        stu.rollNo=1001;
        strcpy(stu.name, "Chandrakant");
        stu.percentage = 80.45;

        printf(" Roll No is: %d \n", stu.rollNo);
        printf(" Name is: %s \n", stu.name);
        printf(" Percentage is: %f \n", stu.percentage);
        return 0;
}
```
Output:
 Roll No is: 1001
 Name is: Chandrakant
 Percentage is: 80.449997

Above program uses structure to store and access "rollNo, name and percentage" for one student. Similarly, we can also store and access these data for N number of students using array of structures.

Uses of C structures are listed below,

(a) Structures can be used to store huge data. Structures can act as a database.

(b) Structures can be used to send data to the printer.

(c) Structures can be used to clear output screen contents.

(d) Structures can be used to check memory size of computers etc.

(e) Structures can interact with keyboard and mouse to store the data.

(f) Structures can be used in drawing and floppy formatting.

7.1   STRUCTURE USING POINTER

In C, structure can be accessed in two ways, first one is using normal structure variable and another one is using pointer variable. In the normal structure variable, dot(.) operator is used to access the data and arrow ($\rightarrow$) is used to access the data using pointer variable.

Syntax of a pointer variable of structure is shown in below snippet:

```
struct structure_name {
    member1;
    member2;
    .
    .
};
// Inside a function
struct structure_name *ptr;
```

Here, the pointer variable of type *structure_name* is created. Members of structure through pointer can be used in two ways: one is, referencing pointer to another address to access memory and another is, using dynamic memory allocation.

Consider below example to access members of structure through pointer.

```
#include <stdio.h>
struct student
{
    int rollNo;
    char name[40];
    float percentage;
};

int main()
{
    int i;
    struct student stu = {1001, "Chandrakant", 88.98};
    struct student *ptr;
    ptr = &stu;
    printf("Data of STUDENT: \n");
    printf("  Roll No is: %d \n", ptr->rollNo);
    printf("  Name is: %s \n", ptr->name)
    printf("  Percentage is: %f \n\n", ptr->percentage);
    return 0;
}
```

Output:
    Roll No is: 1001
    Name is: Chandrakant
    Percentage is: 88.980003

In this example, the pointer variable of type *struct* name is referenced to the address of *stu*. Then, only the structure member through pointer can be accessed. Structure pointer member can also be accessed using → operator, for example (*ptr).rollNo is same as ptr→rollNo.

To access member of structure using pointers, memory can be allocated dynamically using *malloc()* function. See below example to use structure's member through pointer using *malloc()* function.

```c
#include <stdio.h>
struct student
{
    int rollNo;
    char name[40];
    float percentage;
};

int main()
{
    int i, n=1;
    struct student *ptr;
    ptr=(struct name*)malloc(n*sizeof(struct student));
        ptr->rollNo=1001;
        strcpy(ptr->name, "Chandrakant");
        ptr->percentage=88.98;
    printf("Data of STUDENT: \n");
    printf("   Roll No is: %d \n", ptr->rollNo);
    printf("   Name is: %s \n", ptr->name);
    printf("   Percentage is: %f \n\n", ptr->percentage);
    return 0;
}
```
Output:
Roll No is: 1001
Name is: Chandrakant
Percentage is: 88.980003

7.2 STRUCTURE WITHIN STRUCTURE

Declaring a structure inside another structure is called as nesting of structures where a structure acts as a member of another structure. The structure variables can be a normal structure variable or a pointer variable to access the member data.

Syntax:

```c
struct structure_name1
{
    //Members
};

struct structure_name2
```

```
{
// Memebers
struct structure_name1 member_name;
} object_name;
```

We can access nested elements using dot/→ operator. 'structure_name1' structure is nested within 'structure_name2' Structure. Members of the 'structure_name1' can be accessed using 'structure_name2', object_name and member_name are two structure variables.

```
#include <stdio.h>
#include <string.h>
struct structure_name1
{
int college_id;
char college_name[50];
};

struct structure_name2
{
int id;
char name[20];
float percentage;
// structure within a structure
struct structure_name1 str1;
} str2;

int main()
{
struct structure_name2 str2 = {1001, "Chandrakant", 89.98, 2001,
"CITECH, Bangalore"};
printf(" Id is: %d \n", str2.id);
printf(" Name is: %s \n", str2.name);
printf(" Percentage is: %f \n\n", str2.percentage);
printf(" College Id is: %d \n", str2.str1.college_id);
printf(" College Name is: %s \n", str2.str1.college_name);
return 0;
}
```
Output:
Id is: 1001
Name is: Chandrakant
Percentage is: 89.980003

College Id is: 2001
College Name is: CITECH, Bangalore

Above example shows a structure within a structure using normal variable, it tells how to use a structure within a structure in C using normal variable. The "structure_name1" structure is declared inside "structure_name2" structure, both structure variables are normal structure variables, hence the members of "structure_name1" structure are accessed by 2 dot(.) operator and members of "structure_name2" structure are accessed by single dot(.) operator.

```
#include <stdio.h>
```

```
#include <string.h>
struct structure_name1
{
int college_id;
char college_name[50];
};

struct structure_name2
{
int id;
char name[20];
float percentage;
// structure within a structure
struct structure_name1 str1;
}str2, *str2ptr;

int main()
{
struct structure_name2 str2 = {1001, "Chandrakant", 89.98, 2001,
"CITECH,Bangalore"};
    str2ptr=&str2;
printf(" Id is: %d \n", str2ptr->id);
printf(" Name is: %s \n", str2ptr->name);
printf(" Percentage is: %f \n\n", str2ptr->percentage);
printf(" College Id is: %d \n", str2ptr->str1.college_id);
printf(" College Name is: %s \n", str2ptr->str1.college_name);
return 0;
}
```

Output:
 Id is: 1001
 Name is: Chandrakant
 Percentage is: 89.980003

 College Id is: 2001
 College Name is: CITECH,Bangalore

Above program shows a structure within a structure using pointer variable, "structure_name1" structure is declared inside "structure_name2" structure in this program. One normal structure variable and one pointer structure variable is used in this program.

7.3   STRUCTURE MEMORY ALLOCATION AND PADDING

The compiler allocates adjacent memory for the data members of the structure if we create an object of a structure. Usually the size of allocated memory is no less than the sum of sizes of all data members. In addition to the above size, the compiler can use padding and given that case there is will be unused space created between two data members. The padding can be done for the alignment of data member which makes the access to the member quicker. The size of alignment is mostly dependent in processor architecture. However you can manage the padding behaviour and can stop compiler to generated extra space.
The structure data members are accessed with the help of the base address of the structure and the offset of the data member in the structure object.

Example:

```
#include <stdio.h>
struct Student
{
int rollNo;
char name[40];
float percentage;
int colzId;
}s1;

int main()
{
struct Student stu;
printf(" Size of a instance stu is %d \n", sizeof(stu));
printf(" Size of a instance s1 is %d \n", sizeof(s1));
printf(" size of stu.rollNo is %d \n", sizeof(stu.rollNo));
printf(" size of stu.name is %d \n", sizeof(stu.name));
printf(" size stu.percentage is: %d \n", sizeof(stu.percentage));
printf(" size stu.colzId is: %d \n", sizeof(stu.colzId));
return 0;
}
```

Output:
```
Size of a instance stu is 52
Size of a instance s1 is 52
size of stu.rollNo is 4
size of stu.name is 40
size stu.percentage is: 4
size stu.colzId is: 4
```

Above program is compiled of 32-bit machine. The sizeof(stu) will give you the size of the structure including any padding bytes, for example should you want to use *malloc* to allocate memory for it. On some platforms where the compiler does not include any padding bytes on which the size of the structure is the sum of the size of its members.

7.4   TYPE DEFINITION

The *typedef* is used to assign alternative names to existing types, a structure type is typically defined near to the start of a file using a *typedef* statement. The *typedef* defines and names a new type, permitting its use throughout the program. typedefs generally happen just after the *#define* and *#include* statements in a file. There are two different namespaces of types: a namespace of struct/union/enum tag names and a namespace of *typedef* names.
If we code like,
struct Student ... ;
Student x;
would result in a compiler error, because Student is only defined in the tag namespace. We need to have declaration as *struct Student x;*
Any time you want to refer to a Student, need to call it as a struct Student. This may annoy while coding and referring, so you can add a *typedef*:
struct Student ... ;
typedef struct Student Student;

Now both *struct* Student (in the tag namespace) and just plain Student (in the typedef namespace) both refers to the same thing and you can freely declare objects of type Student without the *struct* keyword. The construct *typedef struct Student ... Student;* is just an short form for the declaration and *typedef*. Finally, typedef *struct ... Student;* declares an anonymous structure and creates a *typedef* for it. Hence, with this construct, it does not have a name in the tag namespace, only a name in the *typedef* namespace. This means it also cannot be forward-declared. If you want to make a forward declaration, you have to give it a name in the tag namespace.

Example:

```c
#include <stdio.h>
typedef struct Student
{
        int rollNo;
        char name[40];
        float percentage;
} st;

int main()
{
        st stu;
        stu.rollNo=1001;
        strcpy(stu.name, "Chandrakant");
        stu.percentage = 80.45;

        printf(" Roll No is: %d \n", stu.rollNo);
        printf(" Name is: %s \n", stu.name);
        printf(" Percentage is: %f \n", stu.percentage);
        return 0;
}
```
Output:
 Roll No is: 1001
 Name is: Chandrakant
 Percentage is: 80.449997

Chapter 8

Structures and Functions

C Structures can be used as parameters to functions and can be returned from the functions as well. The structure can be passed to functions in two ways: Passing by value (passing actual value as argument) and Passing by reference (passing address of an argument). Apart from this we can have a global structure instance, where changes affected globally. Similarly a function return structure or just structure pointer.

8.1 PASSING STRUCTURE BY VALUE

The entire structure is passed to another function by value. That is passing all members and their values. This structure can be accessed from called function. Since a structure variable is passed to the function as an argument as a normal variable, change made in structure variable in function definition does not reflect in original structure variable in calling function.

Example:

```c
#include <stdio.h>
struct Student
{
        int rollNo;
        char name[40];
        float percentage;
};
void func(struct Student st){
        printf(" Roll No is: %d \n", st.rollNo);
        printf(" Name is: %s \n", st.name);
        printf(" Percentage is: %f \n", st.percentage);
}
int main()
{
        struct Student stu;
        stu.rollNo=1001;
        strcpy(stu.name, "Chandrakant");
        stu.percentage = 80.45;
        func(stu);
        return 0;
}
```

Output:

Roll No is: 1001
Name is: Chandrakant
Percentage is: 80.449997

In the above program, *stu* is structure instance which is passed to a function *func()*, in that function, all structure members are accessed with values.

8.2   PASSING STRUCTURE BY REFERENCE

In the passed reference, the address location of a structure variable is passed to function as passing it by reference. Here, change made in the structure variable in function definition reflects in original structure variable in the calling function.
Example:

```c
#include <stdio.h>
struct Student
{
        int rollNo;
        char name[40];
        float percentage;
};
void func1(struct Student st){
    st.rollNo=2001;
        strcpy(st.name,"Badrinath");
        st.percentage=89.67;
}
void func2(struct Student *st){
    st->rollNo=3001;
        strcpy(st->name,"Vikash");
        st->percentage=99.12;
}
int main()
{
        struct Student stu;

        stu.rollNo=1001;
        strcpy(stu.name, "Chandrakant");
        stu.percentage = 80.45;
        func1(stu);
                printf(" Roll No is: %d \n", stu.rollNo);
        printf(" Name is: %s \n", stu.name);
        printf(" Percentage is: %f \n", stu.percentage);
                func2(&stu);
                printf(" Roll No is: %d \n", stu.rollNo);
        printf(" Name is: %s \n", stu.name);
        printf(" Percentage is: %f \n", stu.percentage);
        return 0;
}
```
Output:
 Roll No is: 1001
 Name is: Chandrakant

Percentage is: 80.449997
Roll No is: 3001
Name is: Vikash
Percentage is: 99.120003

In the above program, you can notice both workings of passed structure by reference and passed structure by value. By observing the output, it is clear that, with reference function *func2()* holds the changes done inside a method and reflected same in the caller function. But this is not true in case of passed by value.

8.3   DECLARE STRUCTURE VARIABLE AS GLOBAL

Here no need to pass any structure to any function, but still a function can access it, it happens only through a global variable. When a structure variable is declared as global, this means is visible to all the functions in a program.
Example:

```c
#include <stdio.h>
struct Student
{
int rollNo;
char name[40];
float percentage;
};
struct Student stu;
void func(){
stu.rollNo=2001;
strcpy(stu.name,"Badrinath");
stu.percentage=89.67;
}
int main()
{
stu.rollNo=1001;
strcpy(stu.name, "Chandrakant");
stu.percentage = 80.45;
func();
printf(" Roll No is: %d \n", stu.rollNo);
printf(" Name is: %s \n", stu.name);
printf(" Percentage is: %f \n", stu.percentage);
return 0;
}
```

Output:
Roll No is: 2001
Name is: Badrinath
Percentage is: 89.669998

As shown in the above program, global structure variable *str* holds the recent updates of the members. Hence you can see the updated values.

8.4   FUNCTION TO RETURN A STRUCTURE

Similar to any other data type returning from a function, we can too return structure variable.
Example:

```
#include <stdio.h>
struct Student
{
int rollNo;
char name[40];
float percentage;
};
struct Student func(){
struct Student stu ;
stu.rollNo=1001;
strcpy(stu.name, "Chandrakant");
stu.percentage = 80.45;
return stu;
}
int main()
{
struct Student st;
st=func();
printf(" Roll No is: %d \n", st.rollNo);
printf(" Name is: %s \n", st.name);
printf(" Percentage is: %f \n", st.percentage);
return 0;
}
```

Output:
 Roll No is: 1001
 Name is: Chandrakant
 Percentage is: 80.449997

In the above program, the function *func()* create a structure and returns to caller.

8.5   FUNCTION TO RETURN A POINTER TO STRUCTURE

It is possible to return a structure pointer from a function. See below example, function *func()* returns a pointer to structure to caller function.
Example:

```
#include <stdio.h>
#include <string.h>
#include <malloc.h>
struct Student
{
int rollNo;
char name[40];
float percentage;
};
struct Student *func(){
struct Student *stu ;
stu = (struct Student *) malloc( sizeof(struct Student) );
stu->rollNo=1001;
strcpy(stu->name, "Chandrakant");
stu->percentage = 80.45;
```

```
return stu;
}
int main()
{
struct Student *st;
st=func();
printf(" Roll No is: %d \n", st->rollNo);
printf(" Name is: %s \n", st->name);
printf(" Percentage is: %f \n", st->percentage);
return 0;
}
```
Output:
 Roll No is: 1001
 Name is: Chandrakant
 Percentage is: 80.449997

8.6 STRUCTURES AND ARRAYS

Arrays of structures is a collection of structures, in other words array storing different types of structure member variables.

A structure and array can be linked in two ways, one is, structure array and another is, array of pointer to structure.

See below example for structure array.

```
#include <stdio.h>
typedef struct Student
{
int rollNo;
char name[40];
float percentage;
} st;
int main()
{
int i;
st str[3];
for(i=0;i<3;i++){
scanf("%d",&str[i].rollNo);
scanf("%s",&str[i].name);
scanf("%f",&str[i].percentage);
}
for(i=0;i<3;i++){
printf(" Roll No is: %d \n", str[i].rollNo);
printf(" Name is: %s \n", str[i].name);
printf(" Percentage is: %f \n", str[i].percentage);
}
return 0;
}
```
Input:
1
Badrinath

99.78
2
Chandrakant
99.78
3
Suresh
99.78

Output:
```
 Roll No is: 1
 Name is: Badrinath
 Percentage is: 99.779999
 Roll No is: 2
 Name is: Chandrakant
 Percentage is: 99.779999
 Roll No is: 3
 Name is: Suresh
 Percentage is: 99.779999
```

Above program is used to store and access "Roll No, Name and Percentage" for 3 students. Structure array can be used to store and display records for many students. We can store N number of students record by declaring structure variable as "st str[n]", where n can be any number etc.

In array of pointer to structure, Structures elements are stored in the memory and there base addresses are stored in pointers. This will reduce the accessing time of structures. Dynamic Memory Allocation is used in this case. See below example,

```c
#include <stdio.h>
struct Student
{
            int rollNo;
            char name[40];
            float percentage;
} *str[3];
int main()
{
            int i;
            for(i=0;i<3;i++){
            str[i] = (struct Student *) malloc(sizeof(struct Student));
            scanf("%d",&str[i]->rollNo);
            scanf("%s",&str[i]->name);
            scanf("%f",&str[i]->percentage);
}
for(i=0;i<3;i++){
            printf(" Roll No is: %d \n", str[i]->rollNo);
            printf(" Name is: %s \n", str[i]->name);
            printf(" Percentage is: %f \n", str[i]->percentage);
}

            return 0;
}
```
Input:

```
1
Badrinath
99.78
2
Chandrakant
99.78
3
Suresh
99.78
```

Output:
```
Roll No is: 1
Name is: Badrinath
Percentage is: 99.779999
Roll No is: 2
Name is: Chandrakant
Percentage is: 99.779999
Roll No is: 3
Name is: Suresh
Percentage is: 99.779999
```

In this program too used to store and access "Roll No, Name and Percentage" for 3 students. Similar to previous Structure, array can be used to store and display records for many students. We can store N number of students record by declaring structure variable as "*str[n]", where n can be any number etc.

Chapter 9

Unions and Typedef

9.1 UNION

Union is similar to structure, it is a another kind of data type with two or more element but all the members share a common memory location in the union. The union size considers the size of largest member. Since the union member allocates a common location they have the same starting address. But a structure will have different memory locations for each data type member. The purpose of unions is to stay away from memory fragmentation by arranging for a standard size for data in the memory. When dynamically allocated memory is freed, it can be reusable by another instance of the same type of union. A union is declared similar to a structure. The keyword used for Union is *union*. The syntax of union declaration is as follows,

```
union  union_name
        {
          Data_type  element  1;
          Data_type  element  2;

          Data_type  element  n;
        };
```

9.2 DIFFERENCE BETWEEN STRUCTURE AND UNION

Main difference is highlighted in figure 15.1, unions are conceptually identical to structure except storage space for members. All the differences are listed in table 9.1.

Structure	Union
Structure allocates storage space for all its members separately.	Union allocates one memory space for all its members, it finds that which of its member requires high storage space over other members and allocates that much space.
Structure needs higher memory space.	Union needs lower memory space over structure.
We can access all members of structure at a time.	We can access only one member of union at a time.
All members may be initialized.	Only first member may be initialized.

Consume more memory space than union.	Conservation of memory is possible.

Syntax:
 	
``struct struct_name
{
    Data_type element 1;
    Data_type element 2;
    ..
    Data_type element n;
}```
	Syntax:
	
	``union union_name
	  {
	      Data_type element 1;
	      Data_type element 2;
	      ..
	      Data_type element n;
	  }```

Table 9.1 Structure V/S Union

9.3 ACCESSING UNION MEMBERS

The member of unions can be accessed in similar manner as that structure. Say below example,

```
union college{
  char name[50];
  int code;
};
//Inside a Function
union college c1, c2, *c3;
```

In the above code, union variables c1, c2 and union pointer variable c3 of type union college is created. If we you want to access *code* for union variable *c1* in above example, it can be accessed as *c1.code*. If you want to access *code* for union pointer variable *c3*, it can be accessed as *(*c3).code* or as *c3→code*.

Table 9.2 shows normal variable and pointer variables details like syntax of union, declare a union, initializing and accessing the members of the union.

Type	Using normal variable	Using pointer variable

Syntax	```union union_tag_name
	{
	data type union_var1;
	data type union_var2;
	data type union_var3;
	};```
		``union union_tag_name
		{
		data type union_var1;
		data type union_var2;
		data type union_var3;
		};```

Example	union college
	{
	int code;
	char name[100];
	float passAvg;
	};
		union college
		{
		int code;
		char name[100];
		float passAvg;
		};

Declaring union variable	union college colVar;	union college *colVar, rep;
Initializing union variable	union college colVar = {1001, "CITECH, Bangalore", 99.99};	union college rep = {1001, "CITECH, Bangalore", 99.99}; colVar = &rep;
Accessing union members	colVar.code colVar.name colVar.passAvg	colVar → code colVar → name colVar → passAvg

Table 9.2 Accessing Union Variables

9.4 UNION PASSING TO FUNCTIONS

Similar to structure, entire union can be passed to another *function by value*. That is passing all members and their values(few variables will have garbage value). This union can be accessed from called function. Since a union variable is passed to the function as an argument as a normal variable, change made in union variable in function definition does not reflect in original union variable in the calling function.

Example: Passing union by value

```
#include <stdio.h>
union Student
{
        int rollNo;
        char name[40];
        float percentage;
};
void func(union Student st){
        printf(" Roll No is: %d \n", st.rollNo);
        printf(" Name is: %s \n", st.name);
        printf(" Percentage is: %f \n", st.percentage);
}
int main()
{
        union Student stu;
        stu.rollNo=1001;
        strcpy(stu.name, "Chandrakant");
        stu.percentage = 80.45;
        func(stu);
```

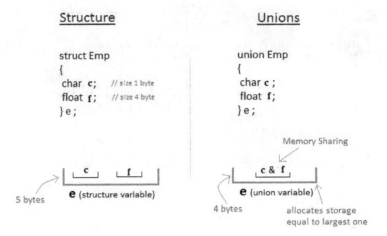

Figure 9.1 Structure V/S Union

```
        return 0;
}
Output:
 Roll No is: GARBAGE_VALUE
 Name is: GARBAGE_VALUE
 Percentage is: 80.449997
```

Here, we can see that values of *rollNo* and *name* members of union got corrupted because final value assigned to the variable has overwritten the memory location and this is the reason that the value of *percentage* member is getting displayed very well.

In the *passed reference*, the address location of a union variable is passed to function as passing it by reference. Here, change made in the union variable in function definition reflects in original union variable in the calling function.

Example: Passing union by reference

```
#include <stdio.h>
union Student
{
        int rollNo;
        char name[40];
        float percentage;
};
void func1(union Student st){
    st.rollNo=2001;
        strcpy(st.name,"Badrinath");
        st.percentage=89.67;
}
void func2(union Student *st){
    st->rollNo=3001;
        strcpy(st->name,"Vikash");
        st->percentage=99.12;
}
```

```
int main()
{
            union Student stu;
            stu.rollNo=1001;
            strcpy(stu.name, "Chandrakant");
            stu.percentage = 80.45;
            func1(stu);
                    printf(" Roll No is: %d \n", stu.rollNo);
            printf(" Name is: %s \n", stu.name);
            printf(" Percentage is: %f \n", stu.percentage);
                    func2(&stu);
                    printf(" Roll No is: %d \n", stu.rollNo);
            printf(" Name is: %s \n", stu.name);
            printf(" Percentage is: %f \n", stu.percentage);
            return 0;
}
```

Output:
```
 Roll No is: GARBAGE_VALUE
 Name is:  GARBAGE_VALUE
 Percentage is: 80.449997
 Roll No is:  GARBAGE_VALUE
 Name is:  GARBAGE_VALUE
 Percentage is: 99.120003
```

9.5 UNION RETURNING FROM FUNCTIONS

Similar to any other data type returning from a function, we can too return union variable. In the below program, the function *func()* create a union and returns to caller.
Example:

```
#include <stdio.h>
  union Student
  {
  int rollNo;
  char name[40];
  float percentage;
  };
  union Student func(){
  union Student stu ;
  stu.rollNo=1001;
  strcpy(stu.name, "Chandrakant");
  stu.percentage = 80.45;
  return stu;
  }
  int main()
  {
  union Student st;
  st=func();
  printf(" Roll No is: %d \n", st.rollNo);
  printf(" Name is: %s \n", st.name);
```

```
        printf(" Percentage is: %f \n", st.percentage);
        return 0;
        }
```
Output:
 Roll No is: GARBAGE_VALUE
 Name is: GARBAGE_VALUE
 Percentage is: 80.449997

Function to return a pointer to union, it is possible to return a union pointer from a function. See below example, function *func()* returns a pointer to union to caller function.
Example:

```
    #include <stdio.h>
    #include <string.h>
    #include <malloc.h>
    union Student
    {
    int rollNo;
    char name[40];
    float percentage;
    };
    union Student *func(){
    union Student *stu ;
    stu = (union Student *) malloc( sizeof(union Student) );
    stu->rollNo=1001;
    strcpy(stu->name, "Chandrakant");
    stu->percentage = 80.45;
    return stu;
    }
    int main()
    {
    union Student *st;
    st=func();
    printf(" Roll No is: %d \n", st->rollNo);
    printf(" Name is: %s \n", st->name);
    printf(" Percentage is: %f \n", st->percentage);
    return 0;
    }
```
Output:
 Roll No is: GARBAGE_VALUE
 Name is: GARBAGE_VALUE
 Percentage is: 80.449997

9.6   UNION INSIDE STRUCTURE AND VICE-VERSA

Below program shows the use of a structure inside a Union.
Example:

```
#include<stdio.h>
void main() {
    struct Student {
```

```
        char name[40];
        int rollno;
        float percentage;
    };
    union ext {
        int age;
        struct Student st;
    };
    union ext u1;
    u1.age=33;
    strcpy(u1.st.name,"Chandrakant");
    u1.st.rollno=1001;
    u1.st.percentage=99.99;
    printf("\n Name : %s", u1.st.name);
    printf("\n Rollno : %d", u1.st.rollno);
    printf("\n Percentage : %f", u1.st.percentage);
    printf("\n Age: %d", u1.age);
}
```
Output:
 Name : Chandrakant
 Rollno : 1001
 Percentage : 99.989998
 Age: GARBAGE_VALUE

Below program shows the use of a union inside a structure.
Example:

```
#include<stdio.h>
void main() {
    union ext {
        char name[40];
        int rollno;
        float percentage;
    };
    struct Student {
        int age;
        union ext st;
    };
    struct Student u1;
    u1.age=33;
    strcpy(u1.st.name,"Chandrakant");
    u1.st.rollno=1001;
    u1.st.percentage=99.99;
    printf("\n Name : %s", u1.st.name);
    printf("\n Rollno : %d", u1.st.rollno);
    printf("\n Percentage : %f", u1.st.percentage);
    printf("\n Age: %d", u1.age);
}
```
Output:
 Name : GARBAGE_VALUE
 Rollno : GARBAGE_VALUE

Percentage : 99.989998
Age: 33

9.7 NESTING UNION

Declaring a union inside another union is called as nesting of union where a union acts as a member of another union. The union variables can be a normal union variable or a pointer variable to access the member data.
Example:

```
#include<stdio.h>
void main() {
    union Student {
        int age;
            union e {
        char name[40];
        int rollno;
        float percentage;
                }ext;
      };
    union Student u1;
    u1.age=33;
    strcpy(u1.ext.name,"Chandrakant");
    u1.ext.rollno=1001;
    u1.ext.percentage=99.99;
    printf("\n Name : %s", u1.ext.name);
    printf("\n Rollno : %d", u1.ext.rollno);
    printf("\n Percentage : %f", u1.ext.percentage);
    printf("\n Age: %d", u1.age);
}
```
Output:
 Name : GARBAGE_VALUE
 Rollno : GARBAGE_VALUE
 Percentage : 99.989998
 Age: GARBAGE_VALUE

9.8 TYPEDEF

As described in structure chapter, *typedef* used to give a new type. A union is similar to a structure in which all members are stored at the same address location. Union members can only be accessed one at a time. Basically union data type is used to prevent memory fragmentation. The union data type avoids fragmentation by creating a standard size for certain data. As in structures, the members of unions can be accessed with the . and → operators.
Example:

```
#include <stdio.h>
typedef union Student
{
        int rollNo;
        char name[40];
```

```
            float percentage;
} st;

int main()
{
            st stu;
            stu.rollNo=1001;
            strcpy(stu.name, "Chandrakant");
            stu.percentage = 80.45;

            printf(" Roll No is: %d \n", stu.rollNo);
            printf(" Name is: %s \n", stu.name);
            printf(" Percentage is: %f \n", stu.percentage);
            return 0;
}
```
Output:
 Roll No is: GARBAGE_VALUE
 Name is: GARBAGE_VALUE
 Percentage is: 80.449997

Chapter 10

Files

A file is a sequence of bytes which is used for storing the data of the users for a long time, file could be a text file or a binary file.

Operations to perform on a File:Creating a new file, Opening an existing file, Reading from and writing information to a file and Closing a file. To read or write a file, we need to perform operations the file via a program as shown in figure 10.1.

10.1 OPENING AND CLOSING OF FILES

We use the *fopen()* function to create a new file or can be used to open an existing file, this function will initialize an type object *FILE*, which holds all the data needed to control the stream.

General form of *fopen()* is:

FILE *fopen(const char * filename, const char * mode); or *FILE *fp; fp=fopen(filename, mode);* here, *filename* is a string literal/name of the file, access mode can be read, write or append, below table 10.1 describes more about modes.

Mode	Description
r	Opening a existing text file for reading purpose.
w	Opening a text file in writing mode, if it does not already exist then a new file is created. Program will start writing content from the beginning of the file.
a	Opening a text file for appending mode(writing), if it is not already exist then a new file is created. Program will start appending content to the existing file content.
r+	Opening a text file for reading and writing purpose.
w+	Opening a text file for reading and writing intention. Before writing, it first truncates the file to zero length if it exists or else create the file if it does not already exist.
a+	Opening a text file for reading and writing purpose. It creates the file if it does not already be present. The file reading will begin from the beginning but writing can only be appended.

Table 10.1 Modes of File

Modes used for binary files: "rb", "wb", "ab", "rb+", "r+b", "wb+", "w+b", "ab+", "a+b".

Opening Mode	Purpose	Status of Previous Data	Syntax/General Form
Reading	File Opened in Reading Only Mode.	Retained	File *fp; fp=fopen("filename","r");
Writing	File Opened in Write Only Mode.	Flushed	File *fp; fp=fopen("filename","w");
Appending	File Opened in Append Only Mode.	Retained	File *fp; fp=fopen("filename","a");

Table 10.2 Opening Modes of File

More details about *fopen* is described in the table 10.2.

To close a file, use *fclose()* function. The general form of this function is: *int fclose(FILE *fp);*. Normally, *fclose()* function returns zero on success, or *EOF* if there is an error in closing the file. Actually this function flushes any data still pending in the buffer to the file, closes the file, and releases any memory used for the file. A constant *EOF* is defined in the header file *stdio.h*.

Example:

```
#include<stdio.h>
void main()
{
 FILE *fp;
 char ch;
 fp = fopen("Test.txt","r");
   while(1)
   {
   ch = fgetc(fp);
      if(ch == EOF )
         break ;

   printf("%c",ch);
   }
 fclose(fp);
}
```

Writing data from a program

Reading data from a program

Figure 10.1 File Operation

10.2   INPUT AND OUTPUT OPERATIONS

Once a file is opened, reading or writing is accomplished by using the standard I/O routines. The simplest file I/O functions are *getc()* and *putc()*. These are similar to *getchar* and *putchar* function and handle one character at a time. Similarly *getc()* is used to read a character from a file that has been opened in read mode. The *getw* and *putw* are integer oriented functions. They are similar to the *getc* and *putc* functions and are used to read and write integer values. These function would be useful when we deal with only integer data. Most complier support two other functions, to be particular *fprintf* and *fscanf* that can hold a group of mixed data simultaneously. The function *fprintf* and *fscanf* performs I/O operation that are similar to *printf* and *scanf* function, except they work on files. Other I/O operations are listed below,

(a) fopen:opens a file (with a non unicode filename on windows and possible utf8 filename on linux)

(b) freopen:opens a different file with an existing stream

(c) fflush:synchronizes an output stream with the actual file

(d) fclose:closes a file

(e) setbuf:sets the buffer for a file stream

(f) setvbuf:sets the buffer and its size for a file stream

(g) fwide:switches a file stream between wide character I/O and narrow character I/O

(h) fread:reads from a file

(i) fwrite:writes to a file

(j) fgetc,getc,fgetwc,getwc:reads a byte/wchar_t from a file stream

(k) fgets,fgetws:reads a byte/wchar_t line from a file stream

(l) fputc,putc,fputwc,putwc:writes a byte/wchar_t to a file stream

(m) fputs,fputws: writes a byte/wchar_t string to a file stream

(n) scanf,fscanf,sscanf,wscanf,fwscanf,swscanf:reads formatted byte/wchar_t input from stdin, a file stream or a buffer

(o) vscanf,vfscanf,vsscanf,vwscanf,vfwscanf,vswscanf: reads formatted input byte/wchar_t from stdin,a file stream or a buffer using variable argument list

(p) printf,fprintf,sprintf,snprintf,wprintf,fwprintf,swprintf:prints formatted byte/ wchar_t output to stdout, a file stream or a buffer

(q) vprintf, vsprintf, vfprintf, vswprintf, vsnprintf, vfwprintf, vwprintf: prints formatted byte / wchar_t output to stdout, a file stream, or a buffer using variable argument list

(r) ftell:returns the current file position indicator

(s) fgetpos:gets the file position indicator

(t) fseek:moves the file position indicator to a specific location in a file

(u) fsetpos: moves the file position indicator to a specific location in a file

(v) rewind: moves the file position indicator to the beginning in a file

(w) clearerr: clears errors

(x) feof:checks for the end-of-file

(y) ferror:checks for a file error

(z) remove:erases a file, rename:renames a file, tmpfile:returns a pointer to a temporary file and tmp-nam:returns a unique filename.

Chapter 11

Dynamic allocations

Dynamic memory allocation in C is to perform a manual memory management through a group of library functions, namely *malloc, realloc, calloc* and *free*.

In the static memory allocation, each static or global variable defines one block of space of a predefined size. The memory space is allocated one time, while your program is started, and is indeed not freed.

As given in the figure 15.1, global/static/program instructions get their memory from permanent area and local variables are stored in the area of stack. Heap is used for dynamic memory allocation during execution of the program.

Dynamic allocation is a special feature to C/C++. It provides us to create data types and structures of any length and size to suit our programs require within the program. This memory is freed once task is finished. This memory also released when you exit the program without a release. Dynamically allocated memory area is secured in a location different from the typical definition of a variable. That memory is called heap but the variables are generally allocated to the location of the stack.

In the automatic memory allocation, memory is allocated as declaring an automatic variable, such as a function argument or a local variable. The memory for an automatic variable is allocated when the control entered into a compound statement having the declaration, and is freed when that compound statement is exited.

In the dynamic memory allocation, memory is allocated on demand through the pointer variables. The C dynamic memory allocation functions are defined in *stdlib.h* header and they are listed in the table 11.1,

Function Name	Description
malloc	Allocates the required number of bytes.
realloc	Increases or decreases the size of the specified memory block. Reallocates as it required.
calloc	Allocates the required number of bytes and initializes them to zero.
free	De-allocates the specified block of memory back to the computer memory.

Table 11.1 Dynamic Memory Allocation Techniques

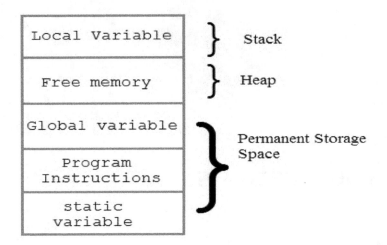

Figure 11.1 Memory Parts

11.1 MALLOC

The *malloc* stands for "memory allocation". This function reserves a block of memory of specified size and return a pointer of type *void* which can be type casted into a pointer of any form.
Syntax: *ptr=(cast-type*)malloc(byte-size);*
Here, *ptr* is a pointer of *cast-type*. The malloc() function returns a pointer to an memory area with the size of *byte-size*. If the memory space is not sufficient, the allocation fails and returns NULL pointer.
Example: *ptr=(int*)malloc(200*sizeof(int));*
Above statement will allocate either 400 or 800 bytes according to size of *int* 2 or 4 bytes respectively and the pointer points to the address of first byte of memory.
In the below example, storing a string by allocating memory of 80 bytes(20*4 bytes).

```
#include <stdio.h>
#include <stdlib.h>
int main()
{
    char *st;
    /* Initial memory allocation */
    st = (char *) malloc(20);
    strcpy(st, "chandrakantn.com");
    printf("String = %s,  Address = %u\n", st, st);
    return(0);
}
Output:
String = chandrakantn.com,  Address = 151748728
```

11.2 CALLOC

The *calloc* stands for "contiguous allocation". The *calloc()* allocates multiple blocks of memory each of same size and sets all bytes to zero.
Syntax: *ptr=(cast-type*)calloc(n,element-size);*
Here, *ptr* is a pointer of *cast-type*. The *calloc()* function returns a pointer to an memory area with the size of

n*byte-size. If the memory space is not sufficient, the allocation fails and returns NULL pointer.
This allocates contiguous space in memory for an array of *n* number of elements.
Example: *ptr=(int*)calloc(20,sizeof(int));*
This statement allocates contiguous space in memory for an array of 20 elements each of size of *int*.
In the below program, 10 numbers are stored in the memory space of equal size.

```c
#include <stdio.h>
#include <stdlib.h>
int main()
{
    int i, n=10;
    int *st;
    st = (int*)calloc(n, sizeof(int));
     for(i=0;i<10;i++)
    st[i]=i;
    printf("Numbers are: \n");
    for( i=0 ; i < n ; i++ ) {
        printf("%d ",st[i]);
    }
    return(0);
}
```

Output:
Numbers are:
0 1 2 3 4 5 6 7 8 9

11.3   REALLOC

If the previously allocated memory by malloc/calloc/realloc is not sufficient or more than sufficient(space waste). Using *realloc* you can change the memory size which is previously allocated.
Syntax: *ptr=realloc(ptr,new-size);*
Here, *ptr* is reallocated with size of new-size. The *realloc()* function returns a pointer to an memory area with the size of *new-size*. If the memory space is not sufficient, the allocation fails and returns NULL pointer.
Example: *ptr=realloc(ptr,40);* Here realloc will allocate memory for 40 bytes.
In the below program, memory is reallocated to 40 bytes.

```c
#include <stdio.h>
#include <stdlib.h>
int main()
{
    char *st;
    /* Initial memory allocation */
    st = (char *) malloc(20);
    strcpy(st, "chandrakantn.com");
    printf("String = %s,  Address = %u\n", st, st);
    st = (char *) realloc(st,40);
    strcpy(st, "chandrakantn.com, CITECH,Bangalore");
    printf("String = %s,  Address = %u\n", st, st);
    return(0);
}
```

Output:
String = chandrakantn.com, Address = 161108088

String = chandrakantn.com, CITECH, Bangalore , Address = 161108088

11.4 FREE

De-allocates the memory which is allocated dynamically by *calloc()* or *malloc()*,*free* explicitly releases the memory space.

syntax: *free(ptr);* Here, the space in memory pointer by *ptr* to be deallocated.

Example: Below program de-allocates the memory which is allocated by malloc.

```
#include <stdio.h>
#include <stdlib.h>
int main()
{
    char *st;
    /* Initial memory allocation */
    st = (char *) malloc(20);
    strcpy(st, "chandrakantn.com");
    printf("String = %s, Address = %u\n", st, st);
    free(st);
    printf("String = %s, Address = %u\n", st, st);
    return(0);
}
```
Output:
String = chandrakantn.com, Address = 151748728
String = GARBAGE_VALUE, Address = 151748728

11.5 DIFFERENCE BETWEEN MALLOC AND CALLOC

All differences are highlighted in table 11.2.

Feature	calloc	malloc
Function	Allocates a memory region large enough to hold "N elements" of "size" bytes each.	Allocates "size" bytes of memory.
Syntax	void *calloc (number_of_blocks, size_of_each_block_in_bytes);	void *malloc (size_in_bytes);
Number of arguments	2	1
Contents of allocated memory	The allocated region is initialized to zero.	The contents of allocated memory are not altered. i.e., the memory contains unpredictable or garbage values.
Return value	*void* pointer (*void* *). If the allocation succeeds, a pointer to the block of memory is returned.	*void* pointer (*void* *). If the allocation succeeds, a pointer to the block of memory is returned.

Table 11.2 Differences and Similarities between *calloc* and *malloc*

We can see the deference between *realloc* and *free* here, typically *free* function is used to release the memory block allocated by malloc or calloc or realloc, and the *realloc* function is used change the size of memory block, this function not only increase the size but data is remain unchanged.

Chapter 12

Preprocessors and compiler directives

Preprocessor is not a compiler part but it is a different step in the C compilation process. Preprocessor is just a text substitution tool which will instruct the compiler to do required pre-processing before real compilation. Generally all the preprocessor commands begin with a pound symbol (♯). It should be the first non-blank character and a preprocessor directive should begin in first column.

A C program involves different processes to reach the final output on the screen, below figure ?? highlights all the processes. Preprocessor advantages includes, easier to develop programs, easier to read, easier to modify and C program is transportable between different systems. List of preprocessor directives are shown in below section.

12.1 MACRO

In some cases we need a condition where we want to use a value or a small piece of code repeatedly in a program. It makes possible a way where one can make the change at one place and it would get reflected at all the places wherever used. This kind of job is done by using a macro. A Macro is defined with a piece of code or a value. Macros can also be defined without any value or piece of code but in that case they are used only for conditional purpose.

Syntax: ♯define OPTIONAL_CODE

Typically, the preprocessor performs textual substitutions on your source code in four ways:

(i) File insertion: Putting the contents of another file into source file, as if you had entered it all in there.

(ii) Macro replacement: Substituting instances of one piece of text with another.

(iii) Conditional compilation: Depending on a variety of situation, certain pieces of your source code are noticed or not noticed by the compiler at all.

(iv) Line control: If you are using a program to collaborate or rearrange source files into an intermediate file which is then compiled, you can use line control to intimate the compiler of where every source line formerly came from.

(a) Defining Macros without values
    Generally we use macros to define them without values and use them as testing conditions.
    Example:

```
#include <stdio.h>
#define M1
```

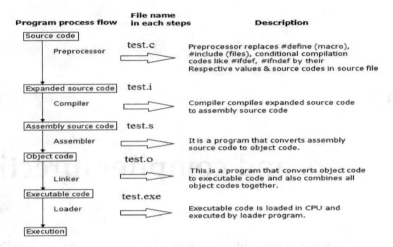

Figure 12.1 Flow of Program Process

```
#define M2
int main(void)
{
#ifdef M1 /* test whether M1 is defined...*/
    printf("\nM1 Defined\n");
#endif

#ifdef M2 /* test whether M2 is defined...*/
    printf("M2 Defined\n");
#endif
    return 0;
}
Output:
M1 Defined
M2 Defined
```

In the above program defines two macros M1 and M2 without any values. These macros are used only in testing conditions. Since both of the macros are defined hence both the *printf* statements executed and displayed accordingly. These type of testing macros are used in a big project having many header and source files. In such big projects, to avoid having a single header more than once a macro is defined in the original header and this macro is checked before including the header anywhere so as to be make sure that if the macros is already defined then there is no require to include the header as it has already been included (directly/indirectly).

(b) Defining Macros through command line

For debugging (or any other feature) purpose in a program while compilation, these kind of macros are used. A macro can be defined through compilation statement from the command line. This macro definition is reflected within the code and accordingly the code is compiled.

Example:

```
#include <stdio.h>
#define M1
int main(void)
```

```
{
#ifdef M1 /* test whether M1 is defined...*/
    printf("\nM1 Defined\n");
#endif

#ifdef M2 /* test whether M2 is defined...*/
    printf("M2 Defined\n");
#endif
    return 0;
}
```
Output:
M1 Defined

Here only M1 is defined but M2 is under a condition. Since only M1 is defined so condition related to M1 executed. Now, if we want to enable or define M2 also then either we can do it from within the code (as shown in above example) or we can define it through the command line. The command for compilation of the code in that case becomes :

```
$ gcc -Wall -DM2 macro.c -o macro
$ ./macro
```

Output of the program,

M1 Defined
M2 Defined

Hence we can see that M2 got defined, then *printf* under the M2 condition got executed.

(c) Macros with values
   There are macros that have some values associated with them.
   Example: #define M1 100
   Here, we defined a macro M1 which has value 100. The name of this macro is replaced with macros value all over the code.

```
#include <stdio.h>
#define M1 100
int main(void)
{
#ifdef M1 // test whether M1 is defined
    printf("M1 Defined with value is %d", M1);
#endif
    return 0;
}
```
Output:
M1 Defined with value is 100

In the above program, a value of 100 is given to the macro M1. While running code, we see that the macro name (M1) was replaced by 100 in the code.

(d) Defining macros with values from command line
   As shown in the previous macros definition, it can be defined from command line, they can also be given values from command line.
   Example:

```
#include <stdio.h>
int main(void)
{
#ifdef M1 // test whether M1 is defined...
    printf("M1 Defined with value %d", M1);
#endif
    return 0;
}
```

In the above program, the macro M1 is being checked and its value is being used but it is not defined anywhere. Lets define it from the command line as follows,

```
$ gcc -Wall -DM1=100 macro.c -o macro
$ ./macro
```

M1 Defined with value 100, so we see that through the command line option -D[Macroname]=[Value] it was made possible.

(e) Macros with piece of code as their values
    Macros can also have small piece of code as their values. Code may be very small and are being used repetitively in the code are assigned to macros.
    Example:

```
#include <stdio.h>
#define MA(a)  a * (a+10)
int main(void)
{
#ifdef MA // test whether MA is defined...
    printf("MA Defined...\n");
#endif
    int res = MA(10);
    printf("Result = %d", res);
    return 0;
}
Output:
MA Defined...
Result = 200
```

In the above program, we defined a parametrized macro which accepts a value and has a small piece of code associated with it. This macro is being used in the program to compute the value for the variable *Result*.

12.2   HEADER FILE INCLUSION

A header file is a file with extension .h which can have C function declarations and macro definitions and to be shared between number of source files. Header file can be written by programmer and files that can come with C compiler. Including a header file is equivalent to copying the content of the header file but we do not do it since it will be very much error-prone and it is not a superior thought to copy the content of header file in the source files, especially if we have many source file containing our program. We can keep all the constants, macros, system wide global variables, and function prototypes in a header files and include that header file wherever it is needed.

Both system and user defined header files are included using the preprocessing directive #include.

Syntax: #include <file>
Generally this is used for system header files. It searches for a file named file in a standard list of system directories.

Another form of include is,
#include "file"
Normally, this type is used for header files of programmer. It searches for a file named file in the directory having the current file.

The #include directive works by instructing the C preprocessor to scan the given file as input before continuing with the rest of the current source file. The output from the preprocessor has the output already generated, followed by the output resulting from the included file, followed by the output that comes from the text after the #include directive.
Example:

```
#include<stdio.h>
int main(void) {
        printf("Hi");
        return 0;
}
```
Output:
Hi

12.3   CONDITIONAL COMPILATION

Set of commands are included/excluded in source program before compilation with respect to the condition. These directives can be used for conditional compilation which controls the compiling of the source code. The syntax of compiler control directive is,

```
#if constant_expression
#else
#endif
```

or

```
#if constant_expression
#elif constant_expression
#endif
```

There are many options used to decide whether the pre-processor will remove lines of code before giving to the compiler. They include #if, #elif, #else, #ifdef and #ifndef. An #if or #if/#elif/#else block or a #ifdef or #ifndef block should be terminated with a closing #endif. The #if directive takes a numerical argument that calculates to *true* if it is non-zero or else its argument is *false*, then the code until closing #else, #elif, or #endif will be excluded.
The preprocessing directives #define and #undef makes identifiers to hold a definite value. These identifiers can simply be constants or a macro function. The directives #ifdef and #ifndef allows conditional compiling of only some lines of code based on whether or not an identifier has been defined.
We can define values and compare those to have variable behaviour with the same define, conditional preprocessor is evaluated at compile time, and conditions using variables are evaluated at runtime.
The *constant_expression* must not contain variables or function calls. If the *constant_expression* evaluates to non-zero, the first part of the program is compiled, the #else part is optional. The #if *constant_expression* section can be substituted by #ifdef identifier.

Example:1
#include<stdio.h>

```
int  main()
{
#ifndef N
printf ( "N not defined..." );
#else
#if N > 10
printf ( "N is more than 10 " );
#endif
#endif
}
```
Output:
N not defined ...

Example:2
```
#include<stdio.h>
#define N 100
int  main()
{
#ifndef N
printf ( "N not defined..." );
#else
#if N > 10
printf ( "N is more than 10 " );
#endif
#endif
}
```
Output:
N is more than 10

Example:3
```
#include<stdio.h>
#define N 1
int  main()
{
#ifndef N
printf ( "N not defined..." );
#else
#if N > 10
printf ( "N is more than 10 " );
#else
printf ( "N is less than 10 " );
#endif
#endif
}
```
Output:
N is less than 10

12.4 OTHER DIRECTIVES

#undef is used to undefine a defined macro variable. #Pragma is used to call a function before and after main function in a C program.

The #undef directive takes out the current definition of identifier. Then the subsequent occurrences of identifier are ignored by the preprocessor. You can also use #undef directive to an identifier that has no previous definition. This makes sure that the identifier is undefined. Macro replacement is not allowed within #undef statements. The #undef directive is normally paired with a #define directive to create a region in a source program in which an identifier has a special sense. The #undef directive also works with the #if directive to control conditional compilation of the source program.
Example:

```
#include<stdio.h>
#define N 100
int main()
{
#ifdef N
printf ( "N defined..." );
#endif

#undef N

#ifndef N
printf ( "\nN not defined..." );
#endif
return 0;
}
Output:
N defined...
N not defined...
```

In the above example, the #undef directive removes definitions of a symbolic constant and a macro. Only the identifier of the macro is given to undefine it.

The implementation of C program supports some features unique to its host machine or operating system. Say, exercise precise control over the memory areas where data is put or to control the way certain functions receive parameters. The #pragma directives gives a way for each compiler to offer machine and OS specific features while retaining overall compatibility with the C.

Pragmas are machine/OS specific by definition, and are typically different for every compiler. Pragmas can be used in conditional statements, to give new preprocessor functionality, or to give implementation defined information to the compiler.
Example:

```
#include<stdio.h>
void One();
void Two() ;

#pragma startup One 100
#pragma startup Two
#pragma exit Two
#pragma exit One 100

void main(){
```

```
printf("\nI am in main");
}

void One(){
printf("\nI am in One");
}

void Two(){
printf("\nI am in Two");
}
```

Chapter 13

Pointers

'C' provides the power and flexibility in dealing with pointers, which serve to set apart from other programming languages. Pointers are variables that hold address of another variable.

13.1   CONCEPT OF POINTERS

Whenever a variable is declared, system will allocate a location to that variable in the memory to hold value. This location will have its own address number.
Example: Let us assume that system has allocated memory location 80F for a variable *a* as shown in Figure 15.1.

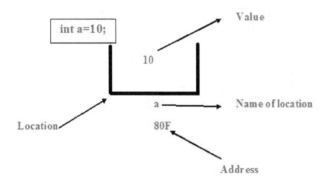

Figure 13.1 Concepts of pointer

We can access the value 10 by either using the variable name *a* or the address 80F. Since the memory address are simply number they can be assigned to some other variable. The variable that holds memory address are called pointer variables. Value of a pointer variable will be stored in another memory location, please refer Figure 15.2. Example: Refer Figure 15.3. **Note:**
⇒ * is an indirection operator.
⇒ The pointer type and the variable which it points to should match otherwise type mismatch occurs.
However to use a pointer 3 steps are required,
Step1: Creation of a pointer:*Declaration*.
Step2: Assigning the created pointer the address.

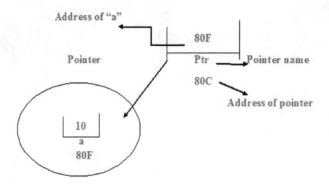

Figure 13.2 Value of a pointer variable

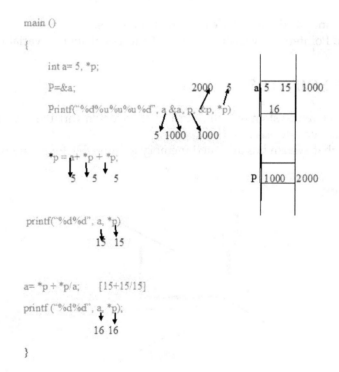

Figure 13.3 Example of a pointer

Step3: De-referencing the pointer access to the data.
Program Example:

```
# include<stdio.h>
#include<conio.h>
Void main ()
{
int num=300;
    int *p; //Creating pointer, this pointer is dangling pointer.
    p=&num; //pointer p is made specific by assigning to it address of number
```

```
printf (%d, *p);
}
```

1. In the above Example: a variable number is created and the value 300 is stored in the variable.

2. Next pointer p is created by declaring p as of type int*.

Note: When a pointer is created, it would be a dangling pointer i.e it would not be point to any variable or would not be containing the address of any variable.

3. The dangling pointer *p is made specific by assigning to it the address of variable number.

4. Now the contents of variable number i.e. 300 can be obtained by De-referencing the specific pointer P i.e. by *p.

5. * Operator acts as the De-reference operator. In 'C' language, * operator has been used for 3 different purposes.

a) To Create a pointer, Example: int *p;

b) To dereference a pointer, Example: *p;

c) To multiply 2 variables, Example: a*b

What is Type casting?

The process of converting address of the variable to the required data type is called type casting pointers.

```
int a= 5;
float *p;
p= (float *)&a;
```

What is Generic Pointer?

It is a pointer which can store the address of different variable of different type but one at a time. In the below example, the pointed data cannot be directly referenced using indirection operator. This is because its length is unknown.

```
void *p;
int a=5;
float b=10.5;
double c=50.555;
p=&a;
printf(%d,*(int*)p);
p=&b;
printf(%f,*(float*)p);
p= &c;
printf(%lf, *(long float*)p);
```

What is Global and Local pointers ?

Global pointers are initialized to Null during computing. Local pointers are not initialized. They are created and used during execution time. Usually local pointers has garbage value. Null is default constant.

```
main ()
{
int *P;
printf(%d, *P);
}
```

Or

```
int *q
```

```
main ()
{
Int *P=Null;
Printf(----, *P, *q);//here p and q points to Null.
}
```

Example:
```
int x=5;
printf(%d, *&x); => 5
printf(%d, &*x); =>5
```

What is Compatibility ?
The pointer type and the variable to which it points to should have same data type otherwise type mismatch error is generated.

13.2   DECLARATION OF POINTERS

Declaration of pointers refers to the process of creating a pointer.
General Syntax:

```
<data-type>   *<Pointer-name>;
```

Where, Data-type is any of valid data type and indicates the type of the variable that the pointer points to. The asterisk (*) is the indirection operator, and it indicates that pointer-name is a pointer variable to type data-type. Since a pointer must hold address, every pointer is allocated two bytes of memory.
   INITIALIZATION OF POINTERS:
It is the process of assigning address of a variable to pointer variable. Address operator & is used to determine the address of a variable. The & immediately preceding variable name returns the address of the variable associated with it.
Example:

```
        int a=10;
        int *ptr; // pointer declaration
        ptr=&a; //pointer initialization
            or
        int *ptr=&a; //initialization and declaration together.
```

Pointer variable always points to some type of data, shown in Figure 15.4. First the variable a and pointer P are created. Initially both the variable and pointer would contain Garbage value. Later the variable a is assigned a value 65 and the pointer P is assigned the address of variable a i.e. 2000.

13.2.1   Dereferencing of Pointer

   Once a pointer has been assigned the address of a variable. To access the value of variable, pointer is deference using the indirection operator.
Example: As given in Figure 15.5, the value 400 can be accessed in 2 methods,

```
i) Printf(%d, num); o/p:400
ii) Printf(%d, *p); o/p: 400 , here *p is accessing
the variable by de-referencing the pointer p.
```

There can be any number of pointers pointing to a variable, at the same time one pointer can point to more than one variable.

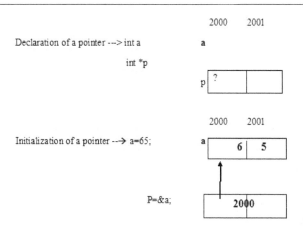

Figure 13.4 Initialization of a pointer

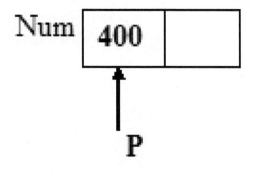

Figure 13.5 Declaration of a pointer

13.2.2 Pointers and Arrays

It is possible to have a pointer which points to any array, example:

```
#include<stdio.h>
int main ()
{
Char a[4];
int i;
for(i=0;i<4;i++)
{
printf(Address of c[%d]=%x\n, i, &c[i]);
}
return 0;
}
Address of c[0]=28ff44
```

```
Address of c[1]=28ff45
Address of c[2]=28ff46
Address of c[2]=28ff47
```

There is equal difference [Difference of 1 byte] between any 2 consecutive elements of array. Let us understand how to create pointers to arrays.

```
int a[5] = {10,20,30,40,50};
```

For the above array, memory is created as shown in Figure 15.6.   2000 is the starting address of array. This

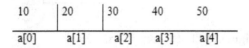

Every memory location would have an address as shown below

10	20	30	40	50
a[0]	a[1]	a[2]	a[3]	a[4]
2000	2002	2004	2006	2008

Figure 13.6 Memory allocation of a array

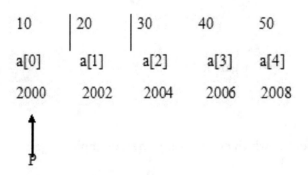

Figure 13.7 Pointer pointing to a array

address is called as "base address" of the array. For the above array "a" pointer can be created as shown below.

```
int *p;
p=&a[0];
or
p=a;
```

The pointer "p" would be pointing to the array as shown in Figure 15.7.

The pointer "p" has the base address of array "a" which is 2000. Once the pointer is created to an array, the elements present in the array can be accessed using pointers.
Example:

```
#include<stdio.h>
#include<conio.h>
Void main ()
{
int a[5]= {10,20,30,40,50};
int *p;
int i;
p=a;
for (i=0; i<5;i++)
{
Printf (%d \t, *p);
p++;
}
getch ();
}
Output:
10 20 30 40 50
```

The increment process of pointer "p" and accessing the element through the pointer continues until all the elements are printed, the process is shown in Figure 15.8.

13.2.3 Pointer to Mulit-Dimensional Array

A multi-dimensional array is of form, a[i][j]. In a[i][j],a will give the base address of this array, even a+0+0 will also give the base address, that is the address of a[0][0] element.

The generalized form of single pointer with multidimensional arrays:

```
*(*(ptr+i)+j) if same as a[i][j]
```

Example: the following statement declares 2-dimenensional array that contains elements of integer type. This array has row and column structure we can consider this 2-dimensional array, arr to be a three-element array, with each of these three elements being an array of five integers as shown in Figure 15.9.
Note: The memory addresses are contiguous row wise.
Example:

```
main ()
{
int arr [3][5], i, j, *ptr;
ptr =&arr[0][0];
for(i=0;i<3;i++)
for(j=0;<5;j++.ptr++)
printf(%u, ptr);
}
Output:
2001, 2003, 2005, 2007, 2009, 2011, 2013,
2015, 2017, 2019, 2021, 2023, 2025, 2027, 2029.
```

Understanding complex declaration:
Compiler interprets complex declaration using right left rule. Start with an identifier in the centre of the

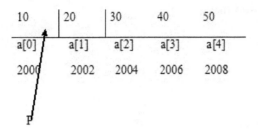

When the statement p++ is executed in the for loop, the pointer p is pointed to address 2002 as shown below.

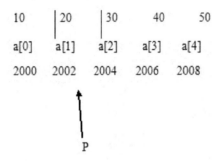

Now when the pointer is defferenced, element 20 is accessed.

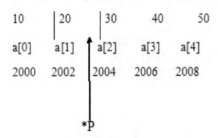

Figure 13.8 Increment of a pointer

declaration and read the declaration alternatively going right and then left until we have all entities as shown in Figure 14.10.

13.2.4   Pointer and Character Strings

Pointers can also be used to create strings character pointers can be used to access strings (array of characters) A character pointer is created as shown below:

```
Char *ptr= HELLO
```

This creates a string and stores its address in the pointer variable str. The pointer str now points to the first character of the string "HELLO". The string created using char pointer can be assigned a value at runtime

Columns

	0	1	2	3	4
0	2001	2003	2005	2007	2009
1	2011	2013	2015	2017	2019
2	2021	2023	2025	2027	2019

Rows

Figure 13.9 Rows and columns in a array

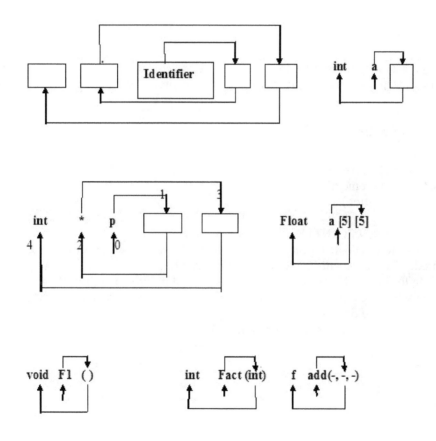

Figure 13.10 Complex declaration

```
Char *str;
Str= HELLO ; //Legal
```

The content of the string can be printed using printf() and puts().

```
printf(%s,str);
puts(str);
```

Note: Str is a pointer to the string. it is also the name of the string. Therefore we do not need to use indirection operator *. We can also have array of pointers. Pointers are very helpful in handling character array with rows of varying length.
Example:

```
Char *name[3]= {
Adam,
Chris,
Deniel
}
//Same program without using pointer
Char name[3][20]= {
Adam,
Chris,
Deniel
        };
```

*char *name[3]*, only 3 locations for pointers, which will point to the first character of their respective strings. Note that memory wastage is more if array is uses; hence it is preferred to use pointers.

13.2.5   Pointer Arithmetic

The 'C' language allows arithmetic operations on pointer variables. The arithmetic operators available for use with pointers can be classified as
1. Unary operators: ++ (increment) and – (Decrement)
2. Binary operators: + (addition)and - (Subtraction)

INCREMENTATION ON POINTERS:
Pointers can be created to int, float, double, char types of data. The pointer created to any of these data types can be incremented. The increment operator (++) increases the value of a pointer by the size of the data the pointer pointing to. In a 16-bit machine, size of all types of pointer, be it int*, float*, char*, or double* is always 2 bytes. But when we perform any arithmetic function like increment on a pointer, change occur as per the size of their primitive data type.
Size of data type on 16-bit machine is shown in Table 13.1.

Type	Size(byte)
Int or signed int	2
Char	1
Long	4
Float	4
Double	8
Long double	10

Table 13.1 Size of Data Type in 16 bit OS

int *i;

i++;

Here, pointer will be of 2 bytes, and when we increment it, it will increment by 2 bytes because int is also of 2 bytes.

float *i;

i++;

Size of pointer is 2 bytes, but now when we increment it, it will increment by 4 because float is of 4 bytes.

Double *i;

i++

Size of pointer is still 2 bytes, but now when we increment, it will increment by 8 bytes because its data type is double.

The size of pointer and various data types is different in a 32-bit machine is of 4 bytes, refer Table 13.2 for other types.

Type	Size(byte)
Int or signed int	4
Char	2
Long	8
Float	8
Double	16

Table 13.2 Size of Data Type in 32 bit OS

Formula:(After incrementing):

New value = current address + i * sizeof(data_type)

3 rules should be used to increment pointer,

1. Address + 1= Address
2. Address++ = Address
3. ++Address = Address

Example: Increment integer pointer

```
#include<stdio.h>
int main()
{
Int *ptr = (int *)1000;
Ptr = ptr +1;
printf(new value of ptr : %u,ptr);
Return 0;
}
Output:
New value of ptr :1002
```

Example:Increment double pointer

```
#include<stdio.h>
```

```
int main()
{
double *ptr= (double *)1000;
ptr = ptr +1;
printf(new value of ptr : %u, ptr);
return 0;
}
```
Output:
New value of ptr:1004

DECREMENTATION ON POINTERS:

The decrement (–) operator decreases the value of a pointer by the size of the data the pointer pointing to.

Example:

If a pointer is pointing to character type of data, then - - would decrease the value of pointer by 1.

If a pointer is pointing to integer type of data, then - - would decrease the value of pointer by 2.

If a pointer is pointing to float type of data, then - - would decrease the value of pointer by 8.

Formula : after decrementing

New-address = (current address)-i*sizeof (datatype)

Decrementation of pointer variable depends upon data type of the pointer variable.

Example:Decrement char pointer

```
#include<stdio.h>
void main()
{
char  a;
char *p=&a;
printf(value of pointer p before decrementation :%u\n,p);
p--;
printf(value of pointer p after decrementation: %u\n,p);
}
```
Output:
Value of pointer p before decrementation   3210648
Value of pointer p after decrementation   3210647

Example: Decrement integer pointer

```
#include<stdio.h>
void main()
{
      Int a;
      int *p = &a;
      printf(value of p before decrementation: %u \n,p);
      p- -;
      printf(value of p after decrementation : %u \n",p);
}
```
Output:
Value of pointer p before decrementation   3210648
Value of pointer p after decrementation   3210646

Example:Decrement double pointer

```
#include<stdio.h>
void main()
{
        double a;
        double *p = &a;
        Printf(value of p before decrementation: %u \n,p);
        p- -;
        printf(value of p after decrementation : %u \n",p);
}
```
Output:
Value of pointer p before decrementation   3210648
V alue of pointer p after decrementation   3210640

Pointer addition
It is possible to add any integer number to a pointer variable. In order to calculate the final value of pointer variable we can use the formula as follows:

Final vale of pointer = current value of the pointer + (integer number * size of the data type);

Example:

```
int * ptr,n;
        Ptr = &n;
        Ptr = ptr +3;
```

Example:pointer to char

```
#include<stdio.h>
void main()
{        char   a;
        char *p = &a;
        printf(value of p before addition: %u \n,p);
        P = p +5;
        printf(value of p after addition : %u \n",p);
}
```
Output:
Value of pointer p before addition   4192755
V alue of pointer p after addition   4192760

Example: increment integer pointer

```
#include<stdio.h>
int main()
{
int *ptr = (int *) 1000;
ptr = ptr + 3;
printf(new value of ptr: %u, ptr);
return 0;
}
```
Output:
New value of ptr:1006

In the above program, *Int *ptr = (int *)1000;* This line will store 1000 in the pointer variable considering 1000 is memory location for any of the integer variable.
Formula:

```
ptr = ptr + 3 *(sizeof(integer))
    =1000 + 3 * (2)
    =1000 + 6
    =1006
```

Similarly if we have written above statement like this *float *ptr = (float *)1000;* the result will be

```
ptr = ptr + 3 *(sizeof(float))
    =1000 + 3 * (4)
    =1000 + 12
    =1012
```

Similarly if we have written above statement like: *double *ptr = (double *)1000;* The result will be

```
ptr = ptr + 3 *(sizeof(double))
    =1000 + 3 * (8)
    =1000 + 24
    =1024
```

Pointer subtraction

It is possible to subtract any integer number to a pointer variable. The final value of the pointer can be obtained from: Final value of pointer = current value of the pointer (integer number * size of the datatype); Example:

```
int  *ptr,n;
ptr = &n;
ptr = ptr -3;
```

Example: Decrementing integer pointer

```
#include<stdio.h>
int main()
{
int *ptr = (int *) 1000;
ptr = ptr -  3;
printf(new value of ptr: %u, ptr);
return 0;
}
Output:
New value of ptr:994
```

Formula:

```
 ptr = ptr - 3 *(sizeof(integer))
    =1000 - 3 * (2)
    =1000 - 6
   =994
```

Similarly for float

```
ptr = ptr - 3 *(sizeof(float))
    =1000 - 3 * (4)
    =1000 - 12
    =988
```

Similarly for double

```
ptr = ptr - 3 *(sizeof(double))
    =1000 - 3 * (8)
    =1000 - 24
    =976
```

Comparison of pointers:

Two pointers can be compared with each other only if both the pointers are pointing to similar type of data. The following relational operators can be used on pointers

> ⟶ Greater than
< ⟶ less than
>= ⟶ Greater than and equal to
<= ⟶ less than and equal to
== ⟶ equals
! = ⟶ not equal

Example:

```
#include<stdio.h>
void main()
{
        int *ptr1,*ptr2;
        int a;
        ptr1=&a;
        ptr2=&a;
        if(ptr2==ptr1)
        printf(pointers are pointing to same data \n);
        else
        printf(pointers are pointing to different data \n);
}
Output:
Pointers are pointing to same data
```

Example:

```
#include<stdio.h>
void main()
{
int *ptr1,*pt2;
        int a,b;
        ptr1=&a;
        ptr2=&b;
        if(ptr2==ptr1)
        printf(pointers are pointing to same data \n);
        else
        printf(pointers are pointing to different data \n);
}
Output:
Pointers are pointing to different data
```

13.2.6   Pointer and Functions

When values are passed to the function, values can be passed or address can be passed. Passing the address is called as pass by reference. This is also called as call by reference. When a function is called by reference any changes made to the reference variable will effect the original variable.

Example : Write a program to exchange 2 numbers, using call by reference

```
#include<stdio.h>
Void exchange(int *p,int *q)
{
Int temp;
Temp =*p;
*p=*q;
*q=temp;
}
Void main()
{
int a =20,b=10;
printf(value of a before exchange is  %d \n,a);
printf(value of b before exchange is %d \n,b);
Exchange(&a,&b);
printf(value of a after exchange is %d \n,a);
printf(value of b after exchange is %d \n,b);
}


Output:
Value of a before exchange is 20
Value of b before exchange is 10
Value of a after exchange is 10
Value of b after exchange is 20
```

Function returning pointer:

A function can also return a pointer to the calling function. The local variables of function does nt live outside the function, hence if we return a pointer connected to a local variable, that pointer will be pointing to nothing when function ends.

Example:

```
#include<stdio.h>
#include<conio.h>
int *larger(int *,int*)
void main()
{
int a = 15;
int b = 92;
int *p;
p = larger(&a,&b);
printf(%d is larger,*p);
}
int* larger(int *x,int *y)
{
If(*x > *y)
```

```
return x;
else
return y;
}
```

Pointers to functions:

It is possible to declare a pointer pointing to a function which can then be used as an argument in another function. A pointer to function is declared as follows: type(*pointer_name)(parameter);
Example:int(*add)();
A function pointer can point to a specific function when it is assigned the name of the function

```
int add(int,int);
int (*a)(int,int);
a = add;
```

Here, a is a pointer to a function add. Now add can be called using function pointer a with list of parameter a(10,20);
Example:

```
#include<stdio.h>
#include<conio.h>
Int sum(int x, int y)
{
Return x+y;
}
Int main()
{
Int (*fp)(int,int);
Fp = sum;
Int s= fp(10,15);
Printf(sum is %d,s);
Getch();
Return 0;
}
Output:
25
```

13.2.7   Pointers to Pointers

It is a form of multiple indirection or chain of pointers. A pointer contains the address of a variable. When we define a pointer to a pointer, the first pointer contains the address of the second pointer, which points to the location that contains the actual value as shown in Figure 14.11.

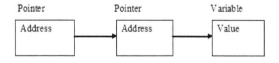

Figure 13.11 Pointers to pointer

A variable that is a pointer to a pointer must be declared as such. This is done by placing an additional asterisk in front of its name.

Example: int **var;
When a target value is indirectly pointed to by a pointer to a pointer, accessing that value requires that the asterisk operator be applied twice.

```
#include<stdio.h>
int main()
{
int var;
int *ptr;
int **pptr;
var = 3000;
ptr = &var;
pptr = &ptr;
printf(value of var = %d \n,var);
printf(value available at *ptr=%d \n*ptr);
printf(value available at **pptr=%d \n,**pptr);
return 0;
}
Output:
Value of var = 3000
Value available at *ptr=3000
Value available at **pptr=3000
```

Advantages of using Pointer :
1. To construct efficient code.
2. To construct compact code.
3. To develop application and system software.
4. To develop different data structure.
5. Using pointer the function can return more than one value.
6. Used in call by reference.
7. Used to implement in dynamic memory allocation.
8. Used for address manipulation and low level programming.

Chapter 14

Introduction to Data Structure

14.1 INTRODUCTION

Data structure is a systematic way of organising and accessing data. Data structures are a way of collecting and organising data in such a way that we can perform operations on these data in an efficient way.

⇒ Data are the facts what we store or preserve.

⇒ Information → Extracted data in the required format.

⇒ Structure → Tools or technique to store data.

⇒ Data Structure deals with, storage of data(efficient method of storing data), accessing or retrieving data in the required fashion, and inter relationship(the relationship between data items in the memory).

A cell is the basic building block of data structures. A cell is some basic or composite data type. Data structures are group of cells representing connections among cells. In simple language, data structures are structures programmed to store ordered data, so that various operations can be performed on it easily.

14.1.1 Types of Data Structure

There are two types of data structures, they are primitive and non-primitive. Using primitive we can operate directly on machine instruction. Primitive [Basic] data types are, Int, Float, Char and Double. Non-primitive [Derived] data types involves, Arrays, Structures , Pointers, Stack, Queue, Linked list, tree, Graph, Enumeration, Union, and so on. Figure 15.1 shows the hierarchy of non-primitive data types.

Array:

Example: *int a[100];*

It is a homogeneous collection of data items. It is also called as subscripted variable. Name of the array is a pointer, which stores the base address.

Advantages of arrays:

It is contiguous memory allocation, accessing is faster.

Address = Base add + Index * size

Limitations:

1. Wastage of memory.
2. Size is fixed.
3. Insertion and deletion takes more time because of shifting.

Need of Data Structures:

It gives different level of organization of data.

It tells how data can be stored and accessed in its elementary level.

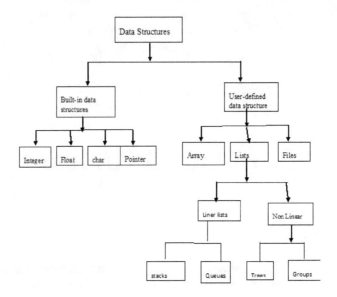

Figure 14.1 Non-primitive data types

Provide operation on group of data such as adding an item, looking up highest priority item.
Provide a means to manage huge amount of data efficiency.
Provides fast searching and sorting of data.

Selection of suitable data structure involves the following steps:
Analyse the problem to determine the resource constraints a solutions must meet.
Determine basic operation that must be supported. Quantify resource constrain for each operation.
Select the data structure that best meets these requirements.
Each data structure has cost and benefits
A data structure require:
a. Space for each item it stores.
b. Time to perform each basic operation
c. Programming effort

14.2   STACKS

It is linear data structure which works on the principle last in first out (LIFO). Here the element inserted at the end will get deleted first. Elements are added to and removed from the top of the stack.

As shown in Figure 15.2, a Apple was the first item(element) that was pushed from top end, secondly orange was pushed, thirdly mango and fourthly banana was pushed from the same top end, finally grapes is also pushed from top end.

One end, called top of the stack. The elements are removed in reverse order of that in which they were inserted into the stack.

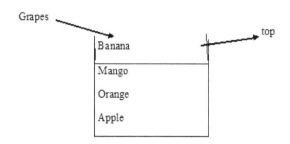

Figure 14.2 A stack of fruits

14.2.1   Stack operations

The basic operations associated with stack.
a. Push():is the operation which is used to insert/add an element into a stack.
b. Pop():is the operation which is used to delete/ remove an element from stack.
c. Disp():printing contents of stack
d. Is Empty: reports whether the stack is empty or not.
e. IsFull : reports whether the stack is full or not
Other names for stacks are piles and push down lists.

14.2.2   Implementation

Stacks can be represented in 2 ways
i. static memory allocation eg: arrays and structures.
ii. Dynamic memory allocation eg:linked list
Static memory allocation: Using arrays
The simplest way to represent a stack is by using a one-dimensional array. eg: stack[n] , where n, is the maximum number of entries. The first or bottom element in the stack is stored at stack[0], the second at stack[1],and the last at stack[n-1]. Associated with the array is a variable called Top, which points to the top element of the stack. To check whether stack is empty, we say "if(top<0)" , if not, the topmost element is at stack[top]. Checking whether the stack is full can be done by "if(top>= n-1)".

A stack containing 10 elements is illustrated in Figure 15.3 in 2 ways one is horizontally and other is vertically.
Note: Stack contains 4 items and its top=3, Stack is declared as int stack [10]

Push operation: Push an item onto the top of the stack insert an item ash shown in Figure 15.4.
Algorithm: Push (stack, top, stacksize, item)
1. [stack already filled?]
If top = stacksize 1 then print: overflow/stackfull, and return
2. Set Top:= Top +1[increase top by 1]
3. Set Stack[Top] = ITEM[insert ITEM in new Top position]
4. Return

Sample code:

```
Void push()
{ int  item;
if(tos = = SIZE -1)
```

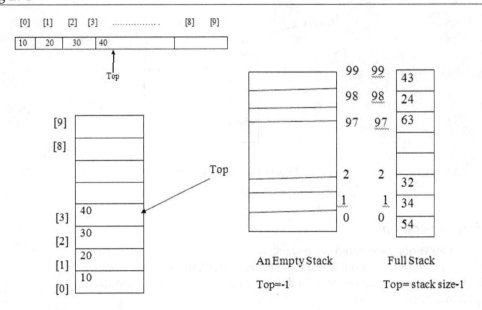

Figure 14.3 A stack operation

```
{   printf(stack overflow \n);
     return;
}
printf(enter the item);
scanf(%d, &item);
a[++tos]=item;
}
```

Pop operation: Pop (remove) an item from the top of the stack as shown in Figure 15.5. Algorithm: pop[stack, top, item] This procedure deletes the top element of stack and assigns it to the variable item 1. [stack has an item to be removed ? check for empty stack] If Top = -1 , then print: underflow// stack is empty and return 2. Set item = stack[top] [assign top element to item] 3. Set top= top -1 [decrease top by 1] 4. Return

Sample code:

```
Void pop()
{ If (tos==-1)
{ Printf(stack underflow);
}
Return;
Printf(elements removed = %d,a[tos--]);
}
Disp()
Prints the contents of stack
Sample code
Void disp()
{ if(tos = = -1)
{ printf(stack is empty \n);
}
```

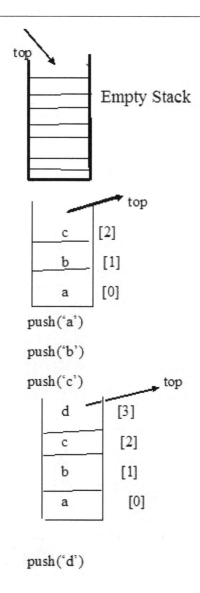

Figure 14.4 Push operation

```
printf(contents of stack );
for(i=0;i<=tos;i++)
printf(%d,a[i]);
}
```

Stack using structures:

```
Struct stack
{ int s[size];
int tos;
};
void main()
{ struct stack st;
```

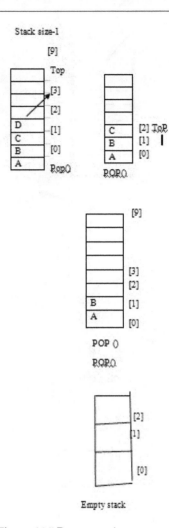

Figure 14.5 Pop operation

```
st.tos== -1;
int ch ;
for(;;)
{ pintf(1.push 2.pop 3.display 4.exit \n);
printf(enter your choice \n);
scanf(%d,&ch);
switch(ch)
{ case 1: push(&st);break;
case 2:pop(&st); break;
case 3:display(&st);break;
default:printf(invalid choice \n);
exit(0);
}
}
void push(struct stack *p)
{
```

```
int item;
if(p -> tos = = size -1)
{ printf(the stack overflow \n);
return;
}
printf(enter the item for insertion \n);
scanf(%d,&item);
p-> s[++(p->tos)]=item;
}
void pop(struct stack *p)
{ if(p->tos = = -1)
{ printf(stack underflow\n);
return;
}
printf(element deleted is %d,p->s[(p->tos)--]);
}
void display(struct stack *p)
{ int i;
if(p -> tos = =-1)
{ printf(stack is empty \n);
return;
}
printf(the contents of stack are :);
for(i=0;i<=p->tos;i++)
printf(%d,p->s[i]);
}
void main()
{
sruct stack st;
st.tos=-1;
int ch;
clrscr();
for(;;)
{ printf(\n 1.push 2.pop 3.display 4.exit \n);
printf(enter your choice \n);
scanf(%d,&ch);
switch(ch)
{ case 1:push(&st); break;
case 2:pop(&st); break;
case 3:display(&st);break;
default:printf(invalid choice \n); exit(0);
        }
        }
}
```

Implementation of stacks by linked lists:
A stack can be represented by using nodes of the linked list. Each node contains 2 fields: data(info) and link(next) The info field of each node contains an item in the stack and the corresponding next field point to the node containing the next item in the stack. The next field of the last node is Null that is the bottom of the stack. The empty stack is represented by setting top to NULL. Because the way the nodes are pointing, push and pop operations are easy to accomplish.

Eg: Program which shows stack represented by linked list.

```
#include<stdio.h>
#include<coniio.h>
struct linked_stack
{ int info;
structlinked_stack *next;
};
typedef structlinked_stack node;
void push (int item);
node *pop(void);
node *top, *stack;
main()
{ node *item;
top=null;
push(20);
push(35);
push(45);
item=pop();
if(item!=null)
printf(\ popped item=%d, iteminfo);
push(65);push(70); push(75);
item=pop();
if(item!=null)
printf(\n popped item=%d,iteminfo);
push(90);
}
void push(int item)
{
stack =(node*)malloc(size of (node));
stack->info=item;
stack->next=top;
top=stack;
}
node *pop(void)
{
node *temp;
if(top==null)
{
printf(\n stack is empty); return(null));
}
temp=top;
free(top);
top=top->next;
return(temp);
}
```

This program can be viewed diagrammatically as shown in Figure 15.6.

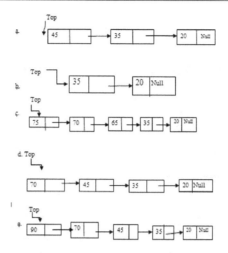

Figure 14.6 Stacks as linked list

14.2.3 Recursion

Recursion is a programming technique in which a function call itself.
There are 2 types of Recursion.
a. Direct recursion
b. Indirect Recursion
A function is said to be recursive, if it calls itself, either directly or indirectly. The recursion process is used for repetitive computations in which each action is stated in terms of a previous result. A recursive function is said to be well defined, if it satisfies the following 2 properties:
1. There must be certain arguments, called base values, for which the function does not refer to itself stopping condition.
2. Each time the function does refer to itself, the argument of the function must be closer to a base value.
Example: Write a recursive function to compute the greatest common driver (gcd) of 2 integers of x and y.

```
int gcd(int x, int y)
{   int g;
if (y<=x  && x%y==0) g=y;
else
if(x>y) g=gcd(y,x);
else
g=gcd(y,x%y);
return (g);
}
The expression x%y yields the remainder of x upon division of y.
The gcd of 2 integers x and y is defined as.
gcd(x,y)=y if(y<=x and x%y=0)
gcd(x,y)=gcd(y,x)    if (x<y)
gcd(x,y)=gcd(y, x%y)  otherwise
for Eg 1:
Let us evaluate recursively the gcd(36,63)
gcd(x,y)= gcd(36,63)
```

```
  = gcd(63,36) as x<y
  = gcd(36,
63%36)=gcd(36,27) as y<x
  =gcd(27,36%27) =gcd(27,9) as y<x
  =9 as y<x and x%y=0
```

Example: Write a "factorial function" explains the recursion. The product of the positive integers from 1 to n is called "n factorial" and is usually denoted by n!

```
n!= 1*2*3*.............(n-2)(n-1)n
```

This is true for every positive integer n, that is n!= n*(n-1)!. Accordingly, the factorial function may be defined as follow
a) n!=1 if n=0
b) n!= n*(n-1) if n>0

Note: This definition of n! is recursive, since it refers to itself when it uses (n-1)!
Example:

```
4!= 4*3!
   =4*(3*2!)
   =4*(3*(2*1!))
   =4*(3*(2*(1*0!)))
   =4*(3*(2*1*1))
   =4*(3*(2*1))
   =4*(3*2)
   =4*6
   =24
```

Stack: Recursive function to compute n!
The items are pushed onto the stack in the following order

```
(4*3!), (3*2!), (2*1!), (1*0!), (0!)
```

The items from the stack are popped in the following sequence: 1, 1, 2, 6, 24 and finally stack is empty.

14.3   QUEUES

A Queue is an ordered list in which all insertions tale place at one end, the rear, Whereas all deletions takes place at the other end, the front A Queue is a first-in-first-out (FIFO) Linear data structure Queue requires the first element that is inserted into queue is the first one to be removed as shown in Figure 15.7.

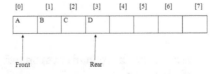

Figure 14.7 Queues operation

Queues are abundant in everyday life. Queue are used in systems to hold tasks that are yet to be accomplished when we want to provide service in a first-come first served basis. Within computer system there may be queue of tasks waiting for the printer, for access to disk storage or even in time-sharing system, for use of the CPU. They are also useful in writing event simulators.

14.3.1   Primary Queue Operations

Enqueue: Insert an element at the rear of the queue.
Dequeue: Remove an element from the front of the queue.
Queue operation is shown in Figure 15.8.

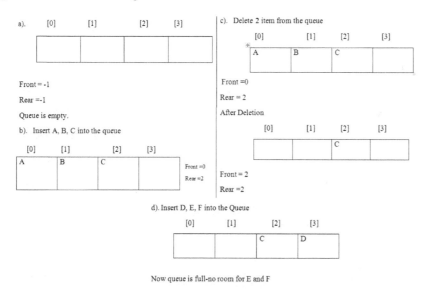

Figure 14.8 Queues operation process

Note: What is happening here is after a sequence of insertion and deletion operations on a queue, the queue tends to move to the last element (n-1) of the array and becomes full even when there are empty or unutilized cells in the beginning part of the array, to overcome this inefficient use of space, we can make the Queue Circular.

14.3.2   Circular Queue

An efficient queue representation can be obtained by taking an array, queue[n] and treating it as if it were circular as shown in Figure 15.9. The elements are inserted by increasing rear to the next free position when rear= n-1, the next element is entered at queue [0] in case that spot is free. That is, element queue [n-1] follows queue.
Example:Write a program that demonstrate the insertion and deletion operations on a Circular queue.

```
#indlude<stdio.h>
#define MAX 5
void insert-qcir(char item);
char delete-qcir(void);
Iint empty(void);
void display(void);
char queue [MAX]; int front =-1, rear = -1;

main()
{
insert_qcir(A);
```

```
insert_qcir(B);
insert_qcir(C);
display ();
delete_qcir();
delete_qcir();
display();
insert_qcir(D); insert_qcir(E), insert-qcir(F); display();
delete_qcir();
display();
}
void insert_qcir(char item)
{
if(front ==0 && rear == MAX-1) // (front==rear+1)
{
printf(\n Q if  Full);
return;
}
if(front ==-1)
front=rear=0;
else
if(rear==MAX-1)
rear=0;
else
rear=rear+1;
queue[rear]=item;
return;

}
char delete_qcir(void)
{
char item;
if(empty())
{
prntf(\n Q empty); return 0;}
item=queue [front];
queue[front]= Null;
if(front==rear)
{
front=-1,rear=-1;
}
else
if(front==Max-1)
front=0;
else
front=front+1
return(item);
}
```

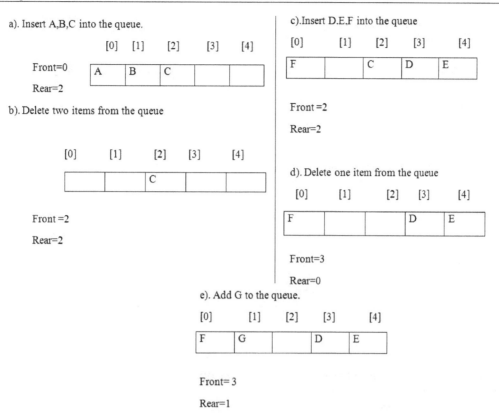

Figure 14.9 Circular queue operation

14.3.3 Double Ended Queue(DEQUEUE or DEQUE)

A Queue is a linear list in which insertions and deletions are made at either end of the list as shown in Figure 14.10. Deque is maintained by a circular array, deque[MAX] with pointers left and right which point to the two ends of the deque.

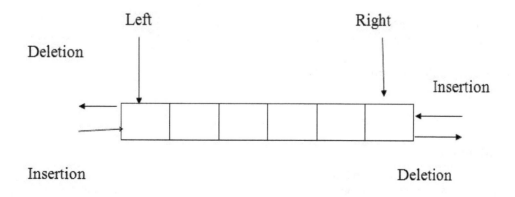

Figure 14.10 Double ended queue operation

Deque can be represented in 2 ways
i) Input restricted Dequeue
ii) Output restricted Dequeue
The input restricted Deque allows insertion at only one end, while an output-restricted dequeue permits deletions from only one end.
The Dequeue can be constructed in 2 ways: they are
i) Using Array
ii) Using linked list
Algorithm to add an element into dequeue
Assumptions: pointer f ,r and initial values are -1,-1
Q is an array
Max represent the size of a queue

Enq_front
Step 1. Start
Step 2. Chek the queue is full or not
Step 3: if false update the pointer f as f=f-1
Step 4: insert the element at pointer f as Q[f] = element
STEP 5 : stop

Enq_back
Step 1: start
Step 2: check the queue is full or not as if(r== max-1) if yes queue is full
Step 3: if false update the pointer r as r=r+1
Step 4:insert the element at pointer r as q[r]= element
Step 5:stop

Algorithm to delete an element from the dequeue
Deq_front
Step 1: start
Sep 2: check the queue is empty or not as if(f==r) if yes queue is empty
Step 3: if false update pointer f as f=f+1 and delete element at position f as element = q[f]
Step 4: if (f==r)reset pointer f and r as f=r=-1
Step 5: stop

Deq_back
Step 1: start
Step 2: check the queue is empty or not as if (f==r) if yes queue is empty
Step 3: if false delete element at position r as element = q[r]
Step 4: update pointer r as r=r-1
Step 5: if (f==r) reset pointer f and r as f=r=-1
Step 6: stop

14.3.4   Linked queues

Linked queues are just as easy to handle as are linked stacks We keep 2 pointers front and rear,
Example: write a program that demonstrates the operations of insertion and deletion of linked queues

```
#include<stdio.h>
```

```c
#include<stdlib.h>
Struct linked_queue
{
Char info;
Struct linked_queue *next;
};
typedef struct linked_queue node;
void insert(char item);
node *delete(void);
void display(void)
node *front, *rear; /* pointers to front and rear */
main()
{
Node *item;
front = rear= NULL;
insertqA);
insertqB);
insert(C);
insertqD);
display();
item = delete();
if(item != NULL)
printf(\n item deleted :%c, item ->info);
displayq();
insert(E);
displayq();
item =deleteq();
if(item!= NULL)printf (\n item deleted: %c, item->info);
displayq();
item = deleteq();
if (item != NULL)
printf(\n item deleted : %c, item-> info);
displayq();
insertq(x);
insertq(y);
displayq();
}
Void insert(char x)
{
Node *new;
New = (node *) malloc(sizeof(node));
New -> info =x;
If(front = = NULL)
{
Front = rear = New;
Front -> next = rear;
}

Else
{
```

```
If(front == rear)
{
Rear = New;
Front -> next = rear;
}
Else
{

Rear -> next= New;
Rear = rear -> next;
}
Rear ->next= NULL;
}
Node *deleteq(void)
{
Node *item;
If(front = = NULL)
{
Printf(\n Q is empty);
Return(NULL);
}
Item= front;
Free(font);
Front= front -> next;
Return(item);
}
Void displayq(void)
{
Node *list = front;
printf( \n linked Q:);
While(list ! = NULL)
{
printf(%c, list ->info);
List= list -> next;
}
}
```

A. INSERTING first Item(A)

```
Front = rear = New;
Front -> next = rear;
Rear -> next = NULL;
```

B. INSERTING second item(B)

```
Rear = New;
Front -> next = rear;
Rear -> next = NULL;
```

C. INSERTING 2 items('C' and 'D')

```
Rear -> next = New;
Rear = rear ->next;
Rear -> next = Null;
```

D. *Deleting one item*

```
Item = front;
Free (front);
Front = front -> next;
```

All above operations are shown in Figure 14.11.

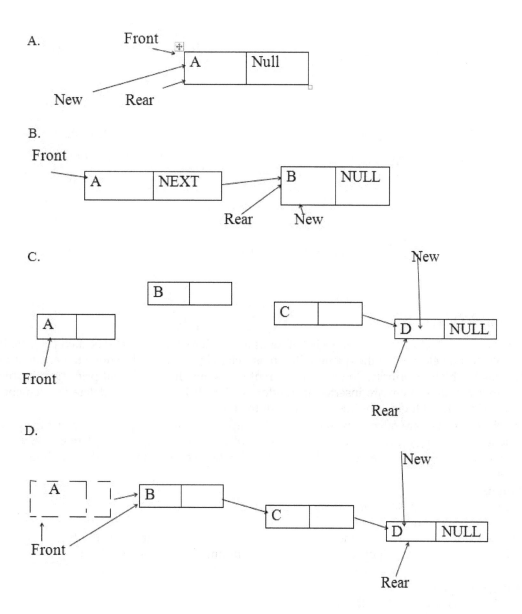

Figure 14.11 Operations

14.3.5 Display operation on Queues

It is the process of printing all the elements in the queue on the screen. Overview scenario is shown in Figure 14.12.

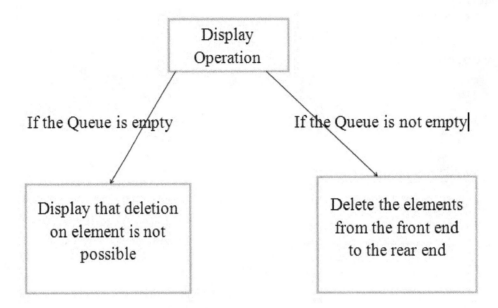

Figure 14.12 Display operation

14.3.6 Priority Queue

It is a linear data structure. It is having a list of items in which each item has associated priority. It works on a principle add an element to the queue with an associated priority and remove the element from the queue that has the highest priority. In general different items may have different priorities. In this queue highest or lowest priority item are inserted in random order. It is possible to delete an element from a priority queue in order of their priorities starting with the highest priority.

While priority queues are often implemented with heaps, they are conceptually distinct from heaps. A priority queue is an abstract concept like "a list" or "a map" , just as a list can be implemented with a linked list or an array, a priority queue can be implemented with a heap or a variety of other methods such as an unordered array.

Operations

Priority queue supports following operations.

a. Insert_with_priority : Add an element to the queue with an associated priority

b. Pull_highest_priority_element : remove the element from the queue that has the highest priority and return it. This is also known as "pop_element", "get_maximum_element" or "get_front_element".

Advantages of queue

1. It is used in job scheduling algorithms
2. It can be used to store data in the first in first out format
3. It is used in printers to store the requests made for printing when the printer is busy.

Disadvantages of queue

1. The main dis advantage is that an ordinary queue might display a "queue full" error inspite of the fact the queue is actually empty.

2. Insertion at the front end and deletion at the rear end is not possible.

Chapter 15

Linked List

15.1   INTRODUCTION

A list is a collection of nodes or objects or data items. The number of nodes in a list may vary dramatically as items are inserted and deleted.

Linked list: It is collection of nodes or data items. Each node contains two fields, an information(info) field and a next address(link) field. The info field holds the actual element on the list. The link field contains the address of the next node in the list. In linked list, the nodes are logically connected. Here, nodes are scattered in the memory but they are interconnected through links.

Example: node1 has address of node2, node2 has address of node3 and so on.

Types of linked list:

a. Singly linked list

b. Doubly linked list

c. Circular linked list: Circular Singly linked list and circular double linked list

15.2   SINGLY LINKED LIST

Here each node has two fields:

1. Info field : to store the actual data (may be divided into sub fileds)

2. Next/Link field: used to store the address of next node.

In singly linked list traversing is possible from left to right only

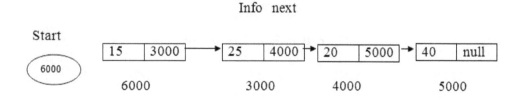

Figure 15.1 Singly linked list

Start pointer: has the address of the first node. The last node next field has null, to indicate the end of the list.

Null pointer: is used to signal the end of a list, list with no nodes empty list or null list.

15.2.1   Operations

The common operations that can be performed on singly linked list are:
a. Insertion: it is the process of inserting a new node into singly linked list
b. Deletion: it is the process of deleting an existing node from singly linked list
c. Display: It is the process of traversing the entire list starting from the first up to the last node and printing the data field of each node during the process.

Insertion:

Insertion of a new node into singly linked list done both at the front of the list and back (rear) of the list.

a. Insertion at the beginning

To insert a new node at the front end of a linked list, we must first create a new node using the malloc() function. After this 2 conditions must be checked.

i. If the linked list does not exist then we must make the newly created node as the first node.

ii. If the linked list already exists then we must attach the new node to the linked list in such a way that the new node becomes the first node

Algorithm:

1. Create a new node
2. Accept data for new node
3. If start =Null, the new node become first node and stop.
4. Insert new node at the beginning and establish the link and start.

It can be diagrammatically in Figure 15.2. *Sample code:*

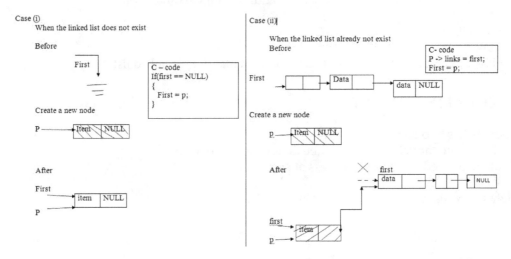

Figure 15.2 Linked list operation

```
void insert_begin()
{
node *new1;
new1 = (node *) malloc(sizeof(node));
printf(enter the information);
scanf(%d,&new1->info);
new1-> next = NULL;
if(start = = Null)
```

```
{
Start = new1;
Return;
}
new1-> next = start;
start = new1;
}
```

b. Insert at rear

First we need to create a new node using the *malloc()* function, after we need to check for two things i. if the linked list does not exist, then we must make the new node as the first node.

ii. If the linked list already exists then we much attach the new node to the linked list in such a way that the new node becomes the last node.

Algorithm:

1. Create a new node
2. Accept data for new node
3. If start = NULL, the new node become first node and stop.
4. Traverse the list till the last node and insert at the end by establishing the link.

It can be diagrammatically shown in Figure 15.3.

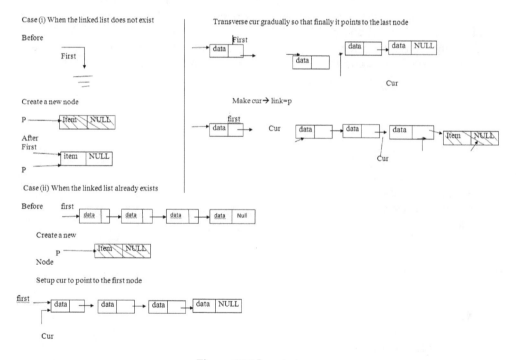

Figure 15.3 Insert at rear

Sample code:

```
Void insert_end()
{
node *new1,*temp=start;
new1 = (node*) malloc (sizeof(node));
```

```
printf(enter the information);
scanf(%d,&new1->info);
new1->next=NULL;
If(start= = NULL)
{
start = new1;
return;
}
while(temp -> next! = NULL)
     temp = temp ->next;
temp -> next = new1;
}
```

Deletion

Deletion of a node can be done from both beginning and end of the list

i. Deletion at the beginning

ii. Deletion at the end

a.Deletion at beginning:

1. If first is NULL, then the linked list does not exist and hence deletion is not possible.

2. If first -> link is NULL, then there is only one node in the linked list. After deleting this node, there would be no more nodes in the linked list and hence first should be made NULL.

3. If first-> link is not NULL, then it means that there are more than one nodes in the linked list., in this case the first node must be deleted and the first pointer must be enhanced such that the second node is now considered the first node(front node) of the linked list.

ALGORITM:

1. If start = NULL

Print list is empty and stop

2. If start -> next = NULL

Print only one node is present

Delete that node, now onwards list becomes empty.

3. If more than one node is present, delete the 1st node, 2nd node becomes 1st node.

It can be diagrammatically shown in Figure 15.4,

Sample code:

```
Void delete_begin()
{
Node *temp = start;
If(start = = NULL)
        {
                printf(list is empty);
                return;
        }
        If(start ->next = =  NULL)
        {
                printf(deleted info = %d, start -> info);
                free(start);
                start = NULL;
                return;
        }
```

Case (i) when the linked list does not exist deletion is not possible

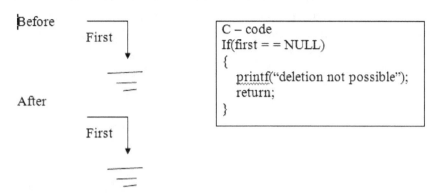

Case (ii) When the linked list contains only one node

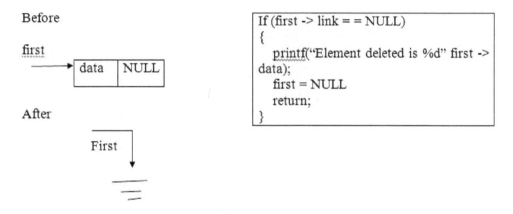

Figure 15.4 Deletion at beginning

```
Start = start -> next;
        printf(deleted info = %d,start ->info);
        free(temp);
}
```

   b. Deletion at the end

i. If first is NULL, then the linked list does not exist and hence deletion is not possible

ii. If first->link is NULL, then there is only one node in the linked list. After deleting this node, there would be no more nodes in the linked list and hence first should be made NULL.

iii. If first -> link is not null, then it means that there are more than one nodes in the linked list.in this case 2 pointers prev and cur must be set up in such a way that the prev pointer is always previous to the cur pointer by one step. The prev and cur pointers must be gradually enhance in such a way that finally the cur pointer must point to the last node and the prev pointer to the before last node. with this arrangement, the last node can be deleted by saying Prev->link = NULL

Algorithm:

1. If start = NULL

Print list is empty and stop

2. If start -> next = NULL

Print only one node is present.
Delete that node, now onwards list becomes empty.
3. If more than one node is present , delete the last node, and next of second last node becomes null.
It can be diagrammatically shown in Figure 15.5,

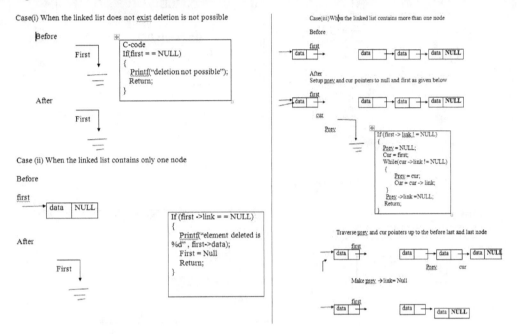

Figure 15.5 Deletion at beginning

Sample code:

```
Void delete_end()
{
node *temp=start, *prev;
If(start = = Null)
{
printf(list is empty);
Return;
}
If(start ->next = NULL)
{
printf(deleted info = %d,start ->info);
Free(start);
Start = NULL;
Return;
}
While(temp -> next != NULL)
{
Prev = temp;
Temp = temp ->next;
}
Printf(deleted info=%d,temp->info);
Free(temp);
```

```
Prev->next = NULL;
}
```

Display operation on singly linked list:
It is the process of traversing the entire list starting from the first up to the last node and printing the data field of each node during the process.
i. If in case first is NULL, then it means that the linked list does not exist. In such a case display operation is possible.
ii. If there are nodes in the linked list, then a pointer called q is set up to point to the first node. It is generally enhanced within the while loop to point to the last node. During the process, the data field of each node must be displayed.
It can be diagrammatically shown in Figure 15.6,

Case(i) When the linked list does not exist

Before

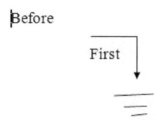

After: Display not possible

Case(ii) When the linked list exists

before

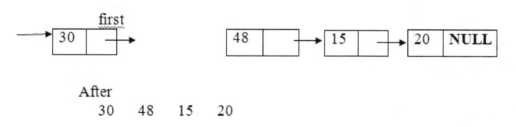

After
    30   48   15   20

Figure 15.6 Display operation on singly linked list

Sample code:

```
Void display ()
{
node *temp = start;
     if (start = = NULL)
     {
printf(list is empty);
Return;
}
printf(contents  of list are);
```

```
while(temp ! = NULL)
{
printf(%d, temp -> info);
temp = temp -> next;
}
}
```

15.3   DOUBLE LINKED LISTS

In certain applications, it is desirable and sometimes necessary that a list be traversed in either a forward or reverse manner. This property of a linked list implies that each node must contain two link fields. The links are used to denote the predecessor and successor of a node. A list containing this type of node is called doubly linked list or two-way-list shown in Figure 15.7.

Here, each node has minimum 3 fields

info field: used to store data(may be divided into sub fields).

lptr/llink: to store the address of previous node

rptr/rlink : to store the address of next node.

Note: First node lptr and last node rptr has NULL to signify beginning and end of the list.

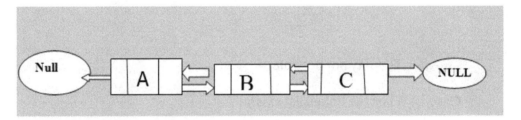

Figure 15.7 Double Linked Lists

```
struct dlist
{      Struct dlist *lptr;
          int info;
          Struct dlist *rptr;
};
typedef struct dlist node;
node *start = NULL;
```

Operations on Doubly Linked Lists:

Insertion: Inserting a node to the list

Deletion: Deletion of a node from the list

Display: Print the contents of the list

Insertion: insertion of a node to the doubly linked list can be done at 3 places a. Insertion at the beginning

b. Insertion at the middle

c. Insertion at the end

Insertion at the beginning

To insert a new node at the front end of a DLL, we must first create a new node using the malloc() function. After this 2 conditions must be checked.

iii. If the linked list does not exist then we must make the newly created node as the first node.

iv. If the linked list already exists then we must attach the new node to the linked list in such a way that the new node becomes the first node

Algorithm:
1. Create a new node
2. Accept data for new node
3. If start =Null
The new node become first node and stop.
4. Insert new node at the beginning and establish the link and start.

sample code :

```
void insert_begin()
{
node *new1;
new1 = (node *) malloc(sizeof(node));
printf(enter the information);
scanf(%d,&new1->info);
new1-> lptr = new1->rptr   = NULL;
if(start = = Null)
{
Start = new1;
Return;
}
new1-> lptr = NULL;
new1 ->rptr = start;
start = new1;
}
```

Insertion at the end:

To insert a new node at the end of a DLL, we must first create a new node using the malloc() function. After this 2 conditions must be checked.

v. If the linked list does not exist then we must make the newly created node as the first node.

vi. If the linked list already exists then we must traverse the list till the end later insert new node at the end by establishing link.

Algorithm:
1. Create a new node
2. Accept data for new node
3. If start =Null
The new node become first node and stop.
4. Insert new node at the end and establish the link.

sample code :

```
void insert_end()
{
node *new1, *temp = start;
new1 = (node *) malloc(sizeof(node));
printf(enter the information);
```

```
scanf(%d,&new1->info);
new1-> lptr = new1->rptr  = NULL;
if(start = = Null)
{
Start = new1;
Return;
}
        while (temp->rptr != NULL)
              temp = temp->rptr;

temp->rptr = new1;
}
```

Deletion

a. Deletion at beginning:

1. If start is NULL, then the linked list does not exist and hence deletion is not possible.

2. If start ->rptr NULL, then there is only one node in the linked list. After deleting this node, there would be no more nodes in the DLL and hence first should be made NULL.

3. If start->rptr is not NULL, then it means that there are more than one nodes in the linked list., in this case the first node must be deleted and the start pointer must be enhanced such that the second node is now considered the first node(front node) of the DLL.

ALGORITM:

1. If start = NULL

Print list is empty and stop

2. If start -> rptr = NULL

Print only one node is present

Delete that node, now onwards list becomes empty. Stop.

3. If more than one node is present, delete the 1st node and establish the link. Now onwards 2nd node becomes 1st node.

```
void delete_begin()
{
If(start = = NULL)
{
Printf(list is empty \n);
Return;
}
If(start -> rptr = NULL)
{
printf(deleted info = %d, start -> info);
free(start);
start = NULL;
return;
}
Printf(deleted info = %d, start -> info);
start = start ->rptr;
free(start ->lptr);
start ->lptr = NULL;
}
```

b. Deletion at End:

1. If start is NULL, then the linked list does not exist and hence deletion is not possible.

2. If start -> rptr NULL, then there is only one node in the linked list. After deleting this node, there would be no more nodes in the DLL and hence first should be made NULL.

3. If start-> rptr is not NULL, then it means that there are more than one nodes in the linked list. In this case traverse the list till the end. Delete the last node and establish the link. Now onwards last but one node becomes the last node of DLL.

ALGORITM:

1. If start = NULL

Print list is empty and stop

2. If start -> rptr = NULL

Print only one node is present

Delete that node, now onwards list becomes empty. Stop.

3. If more than one node is present, traverse and delete the last node and establish the link. Now onwards N-1 node becomes Nth node.

Sample code:

```
void delete_end()
{
node *temp= start;
If(start = = NULL)
{
Printf(list is empty \n);
Return;
}
If(start ->rptr = NULL)
{
Printf(deleted info = %d,start ->info);
Free(start);
Start = NULL;
Return;
}
While(temp->rptr != NULL)
      temp = temp->rptr;
(temp->lptr)->rptr= NULL;
          printf(deleted info = %d,temp->info);
      free(temp);
}
```

Display:

It can be diagrammatically shown in Figure 15.8,

Sample code:

```
void display()
{ node *temp= start;
If(start== NULL)
{ printf(list is empty);
return;
```

Case 1: When the linked list does not exist

Before

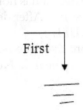

First

After: Display not possible

Case 2:

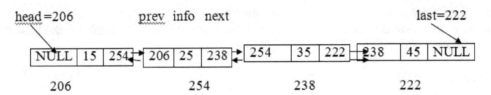

Output
15   25   35   45

Figure 15.8 Display DLL

```
}
printf(contents of dlist are);
while(temp!= NULL)
{
printf(%d,temp->info);
temp= temp->rptr;
}
}
```

15.4   CIRCULAR LINKED LIST

In a circularly-linked list, the first and final nodes are linked together. To traverse a circular linked list, you begin at any node and follow the list in either direction until you return to the original node.

There are 2 types:
a. Circular single linked list b.Circular double linked list
a. Circular single linked list:
It is an extension of single linked list. Here the last node next field has the address of first node. There are ways to implement Circular singly linked list.
Method I: Here last node store the address of first node. Only one pointer is used i.e. start which always points to the first node.
Method II: Only two pointers are used i.e. first and last. First points to the first node and last points to the last node.
Method III: Best method. Only one pointer is used i.e. last, which always points to the last node. Here last

node store the address of first node. Using last->next we get the address of the first node. All above methods are expressed in Figure 15.9.

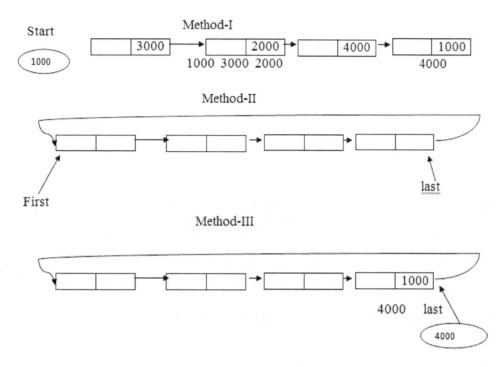

Figure 15.9 Circular linked list

```
struct CSLL
{
int info;
struct CSLL *next;
};
typedef struct csll node;
node *last = NULL
```

a. Circular double linked list:
It is the most widely used data structure. It is an extension of double linked list. Here traversing is possible from left to right and from right to left in circular fashion (clockwise and anticlockwise)
    There are different approaches
Using header node in addition to other node is the best approach.
To simplify the insertion and deletion operation header node is used.

    Header node: is the node which is created first and deleted last. If list is empty the header node is present.
Head ->rptr stores the address of first node
Head -> lptr stores the address of last node
Head -> info may be used to store no of nodes.


```
struct CDLL
```

```
{
int info;
struct CDLL *lptr,*rptr;
};
typedef struct CDLL node;
node *head;
```

Applications of linked list:
Linked list can be used in
1. Polynomial manipulation
2. Linked dictionary
3. Multiple precision arithmetic
4. Representation of sparse matrix and many more

Advantages of linked list:
Efficient memory utilization: The memory of a linked list is not pre-allocated. Memory can be allocated whenever required and released when it is no longer required.
Insertion and deletion operations are easier and efficient: Linked list provide flexibility in inserting a data item at a specified position and deletion of a data item from the given position.
Extensive manipulation: we can perform any number of complex manipulations without any prior idea of the memory space available. (i.e. in stacks and queues we sometimes get overflow conditions. Here no such problem arises.)
The insertion and deletion operation are easy to implement and faster in execution.

Disadvantages of linked list:
1. Accessing is slower. Since traversing is required.
2. As number of nodes increases , the traversing takes more time
3. Each node has one or two links to store the addresses, which leads to memory consumption.(as number of nodes increases , number of links proportionally increases)
4. Tracing and debugging the code is difficult

www.ingramcontent.com/pod-product-compliance
Lightning Source LLC
Chambersburg PA
CBHW060600060326
40690CB00017B/3778